CONTENTS

Introduction: A perennial hunger

CARDINAL PAUL POUPARD
with
Michael Paul Gallagher

WHAT WILL GIVE US HAPPINESS?

VERITAS

First published 1992 by
Veritas Publications
7-8 Lower Abbey Street
Dublin 1

5 4 3 2 1

ISBN 1 85390 134 2

**British Library Cataloguing
in Publication Data.
A catalogue record for
this book is available
from the British Library.**

Cover design: Joseph Gervin
Print origination: Veritas Publications
Printed in the Republic of Ireland by
the Leinster Leader

INTRODUCTION

A PERENNIAL HUNGER

The title of this book is adapted from an ancient religious poem, indeed from the Psalm that the Church chooses for night prayer every Saturday night. In Psalm 4, in the English version of the Breviary, one finds these eloquent and simple lines:

> What will bring us happiness? many ask.
> Lift up the light of your face on us Lord,
> For you have put into my heart a greater joy
> Than they have from abundance of corn and new wine.

On reflection, it seems strangely suitable that Christians are asked to ponder these two contrasting paths to happiness on Saturday night, when so many people around the world opt for "corn and new wine". There is nothing wrong with relishing the gifts of the earth. There is nothing wrong with enjoying a celebration with food and wine: it is suspect only when it suppresses other dimensions of humanity, and becomes trapped "in a web of superficial gratifications" so that people can no longer experience their "personhood in an authentic and concrete way" (*Centesimus annus,* 1991, 41). One of the tasks of these pages is to identify the alienation that is the fruit of such reductive forms of happiness, but its main task will be to point the way to the genuine happiness suggested by that very Psalm. The Old Testament poet writes in praise of a "joy" that is "greater" than the delights of the senses, a joy that comes from God as a gift. That happiness is rooted in the encounter of faith, in seeing one's human life in the "light" of God's face.

Down through the ages this theme of happiness, and how to find it, has been a constant topic for human reflection. Great thinkers of many cultures have placed this issue at the centre of their inquiry into the very purpose of our being here in this world. Thus the question of the psalmist has echoed in different ways throughout the centuries and many varied responses have been offered. Moreover, this exploration has been shared by believers and non-believers alike, for the simple reason that it is such a fundamental *human* quest and question.

This traditional concern, so central in the philosophic tradition from Aristotle to the French Encyclopaedists, has received much less attention in recent times. And yet, perhaps even because of this comparative neglect, it is ripe to revisit this ancient question of human happiness, and in doing so one can find a rich entry point into some major preoccupations of today's world. It is a topic that raises many of the most basic issues facing people now – and it does so on both a humanist and a religious level. In this sense this field of inquiry offers unique common ground for believers and non-believers alike.

Inquiry of the Pontifical Council for Dialogue with Non-Believers
It was because of this richness and relevance that the subject of "Christian Faith and the Search for Happiness" was chosen in 1988 by the Pontifical Council for Dialogue with Non-Believers as its research project for the following three years, leading into its Plenary Assembly held in March 1991. This four-day seminar was preceded by a wide-ranging international investigation. The following questionnaire was sent to episcopal conferences, to Catholic universities, and to groups of believers and non-believers.

1. From the beginning of existence humanity has been engaged in a quest for happiness: what are the characteristics of this search today, what are the forms in which it is expressed, what are the different ways in which our contemporaries seek happiness in the various conditions and situations of their concrete worlds?
2. According to the dominant patterns of thought in today's world, do religions, beliefs, or religious practices help or perhaps hinder progress toward such happiness to the extent that most people feel compelled to search for fulfilment outside of religion?
3. What is the common perception today of the connection

between Christianity, the religion of the "Good News", and human happiness? What is the reaction of humankind to the Christian promise of an eternal happiness in God: is this considered an illusory substitution for true fulfilment on earth, or in fact is it seen as the only true way to satisfy the aspiration for happiness in our world today?

4. How should the Church present the Gospel message in the modern world so that it might truly be seen as a "Good News" for modern times, a "Good News" that is truly able, not only to bring humanity to a sense of eternal fulfilment, but in so far as is possible, to real happiness in this life as well? How might it be possible to proclaim and live faith in Christ so that he can truly be seen by the human family as its supreme hope?

In the three years preceding the Plenary Assembly, hundreds of experts and groups around the world forwarded their insights to Rome. In many countries national committees for dialogue met with non-believers to consider the implications of the theme and to prepare their written contributions. In Japan, for instance, the relevant questionnaire was published in a popular magazine of culture and elicited a few hundred replies from people of many backgrounds and many religious positions. In the year prior to the Plenary Assembly many of these reports were published in the quarterly review *Atheism and Faith,* but the assembly itself was obviously the climax of the whole process.

This event brought together some fifty experts from every continent. These included cardinals, bishops, theologians, philosophers and other experts. In all thirty-five countries were represented at the Plenary Assembly. Those present heard about the faith situations in many different contexts and cultures. They heard directly from representatives from Europe, West and East, from America North and South, from Australia, Africa, India, Bangladesh, Japan and the Philippines. In addition the Assembly received reports on China and the Soviet Union. Fascinating contrasts emerged, and yet in spite of so much diversity, there were many common features.

Not only is the search for happiness something fundamental in all ages and in all people: it is *the* desire of the human heart. At its deepest it is a desire to love and be loved. Ultimately it is the desire for God. Through all history, however, this great vision has run into trouble in practice, and never more so than in today's complex culture when the transcendent goals and horizons of happiness are often lost sight of or trivialised. To reflect on happiness is to touch on one of the crisis points of our age, and it is a crisis that involves both personal life and whole societies. It is also central to the crisis of religious faith in our time. Indeed, the Christian message offers an invitation to a different kind of happiness, a good news announced by Christ and made transparent in him. Many a non-believer cannot see Christianity as a source of happiness, and may even judge it to be a source of illusion and of unhappiness. Even for people who have been born into Christianity, it is sadly frequent that they may not have really heard that call of Christ as a call to happiness.

The religious dimension

> A Christian is not a person of negation, of refusal, of rebellion, but a person who says Yes, who affirms the world, things, life itself. This is the first happiness of the Christian.
>
> Franc Rodé (Slovenian theologian, Pontifical Council for Dialogue with Non-Believers)

> The idea of happiness had a very long history. Each metamorphosis reflected the changing climate of a different social epoch.
>
> Peter Quennell (British writer)

If this link with happiness is lacking, then faith has not been encountered in its liberating fullness. If the essential link between religion and happiness is not experienced, then a gap opens up between how life is lived and how religion is perceived. This pastorally tragic gap is the source of much alienation from faith and much loss of roots by people in our contemporary cultures. It is no exaggeration to say that the crisis of faith today is a human crisis rather than a theological one: it happens when people no longer sense the truths of faith as touching their hearts or as meeting the hungers of their humanity.

How is happiness understood and sought after today? This question is the starting point for this book, but it does not express the full hope of these pages. From listening to the tone of today's humanity, a listening that included believers and non-believers alike, the larger hope is to assist that new evangelisation which today's world requires in so many diverse ways. At its core this will entail an evangelisation of desire, in the sense of putting our longing for happiness in touch with the beatitude of the gospels.

So these chapters have been born of a learning and a listening to many voices, but their larger aim is to serve that renewal in the language of faith which is one of the urgent pastoral needs of today. This book cannot do justice to all the detailed richness of the contributions received – either in the preparatory period when so many penetrating papers were forwarded to this Pontifical Council, or during the four pleasantly crowded days of discourses and discussions that formed the Plenary Assembly. Instead its approach will draw selectively on that accumulation of insights. Its purpose is pastoral, and its hope is to offer a short synthesis concerning the links between happiness and Christian faith.

Three parts

> There is no duty we so much underrate as the duty of being happy.
>
> Robert Louis Stevenson (Nineteenth century writer)

> Christian faith helps humanity to understand itself in a comprehensive rather than a reductive way.
>
> Bishop Anton Schlembach (Germany)

The particular structure chosen for this book is intended to mirror the various forms of dialogue that lie behind it. Thus, in **Part One** each chapter offers different angles on the question of happiness, and the sequence of these short chapters is meant to offer the reader a diversity of perspectives – almost like a kinetic work of art that can be looked at in various ways.

In what does happiness consist? Is it a state of mind? Is it an attitude of heart? Is it fragile or is it lasting? Is it born of human choice? Is it the outcome of action? Is it the fruit of self-giving? Is it rooted in relationships?

Part Two will draw on the wealth of international insights that came to the Pontifical Council both in the form of written commentaries and through those who attended the Plenary Assembly from such a diversity of backgrounds. Because of their contributions to the debate one can move on to questions wider than the personal: Is happiness conditioned by culture? Does it change with history? Is it a social product? Does it differ from country to country? Has it a new tone in the contemporary world? Is it in crisis in new and different ways at present?

Later, **Part Three** will confront more specifically Christian and pastoral questions. Is happiness promised by Christ? Is it the same as the "beatitude" or "joy" of the gospels? Is it a gift of the Spirit? Is it a sharing with God? How might a ministry of Christian happiness meet today's pastoral needs?

This cascade of questions captures something of the range of reflections involved. The chapters that follow will explore these issues, but gradually it is hoped that from these individual parts a larger vision will build up, one that can suggest the crucial relevance of this theme of happiness both for human values and for Christian faith today. As the topic unfolds from the personal through the cultural to the spiritual and pastoral – the individual chapters are intended to accumulate into a more rounded treatment of this whole area, and to move from human perspectives towards more specifically religious horizons.

Throughout the book the reader will find quotations from many authors. Some are from those who contributed to the research of the Pontifical Council. Others are drawn from people who did not have the chance to send their contribution directly – such as St Augustine or Shakespeare! The overall aim of these quotations is to act both as food for reflection for the reader and as an indication of the abundance of response that this whole topic provokes.

Most of all, the tone of this book is meant to be such as would offer stimulation to the non-believer as well as spiritual nourishment to the believer. In this way it seeks to be a book both born of dialogue and fostering dialogue. At its simplest it is a book that tackles again one of the great perennial concerns – how to find a happiness worthy of our full humanity. Finding such a happiness will lead beyond the deep drama of human happiness towards that other happiness revealed uniquely in the humanity of Jesus Christ, Son of God and Son of the Blessed Virgin Mary.

I am happy to have shared the joy of preparing this work with the staff of the Pontifical Council for Dialogue with Non-Believers, and in a particular way with an Irish priest, Father Michael Paul Gallagher, who was formerly a lecturer at University College, Dublin, and is now working with the Dicastery in Rome.

Other language editions of this book will appear in French (Mame), Italian (Piemme), Spanish (Herder) and Portuguese (Instituto de Desenvolvimento Cultural). The English text has come from Fr Gallagher's flowing pen. To him my best gratitude.

Paul Cardinal Poupard

The joyous feast of the Epiphany, 1992

Part One

HAPPINESS AS PERSONAL QUEST

1

HAPPINESS BEYOND THE SURFACE

Man's unhappiness comes of his greatness. It is because there is an Infinite in him, which with all his cunning he cannot quite bury under the Finite.
                    Thomas Carlyle (Nineteenth century writer)

I love and am beloved, and I am happy.
                    Samuel Taylor Coleridge (English Romantic poet)

In the flow of everyday life what does happiness mean for people? The answer to this depends greatly on whether one approaches the question from the outside or from within a person's experience. Certainly from an external point of view it is possible to think of people as living for superficial pleasures and as sadly caught into that level of existence. In so far as this is so, happiness is reduced to something transitory. But within each person is another wavelength, even if it can lie dormant for years, and even if it seldom finds explicit expression. This other dimension within everybody seeks a different and deeper happiness.

One can imagine stopping people in the street and, almost like a newspaper reporter or someone doing a social survey, questioning them about whether they are happy. The first and spontaneous answers might simply identify happiness with "having a good time", or some other external measurement such as wealth, or job satisfaction, or success of various kinds. But if time is taken and if the questioning goes a little further, another level of response would emerge. Invited to reflect more seriously, people will usually move from thinking of happiness as external self-satisfaction, and will discover instead that their real hopes focus on happiness of a different kind. Many of the responses to the questionnaire – as given in the Introduction – described how people often lack the language to express their longings. It is easy to speak of externals. They may be more shy to speak of what their hearts desire.

In what direction do these hidden hopes point? Towards relationships. Towards a sense of self-worth. Towards finding love. There are many ways of expressing this other level of the search for happiness that underlies the everyday life of many an ordinary person. For the moment it is enough to indicate its existence and its central importance.

> A feeling granted everyone
> Of living in two worlds
> One of which is unsayable.
>
> Charles Simic (Australian poet)

> I were but little happy if I could say how much.
>
> William Shakespeare

If again one imagines questioning the person in the street about whether they feel happy, another contrast of levels will arise. A person may initially identify "being happy" with the mood of the moment, and this is another unstable way of measuring it. Small events can cast long shadows. Some disappointment in a friendship, some tension at work, some inconvenience as tiny as missing a bus, a minor illness or a state of fatigue – all these experiences and many others can influence a person's immediate and felt happiness. In an opposite direction, small events of a positive kind can cause a person's mood to swing upwards. A word of praise, a sense of achievement, a pleasant conversation, enjoying a film or a concert, time to relax without pressure – the list could be lengthened almost indefinitely, but the effect would be the same. A person's felt happiness is so easily expanded or deflated by the minor events of each day.

Deeper than moods

Moods are part of the flux of life. They are part of everyone's experience in the adventure of happiness and unhappiness. But, rather like the external yardstick of pleasure, they are ultimately secondary in the search for happiness. The immediate situation

18

may be very real for a person but the truth about happiness is always more than the mood of the moment. Certainly, happiness involves such feelings and is helped by them, but it is not dependent on them for its existence or survival. An inevitable flux of moods need not rock the fortress of genuine happiness, because this has more solid foundations than the transitory. Almost like the coming of storm clouds into a sunny sky, the arrival of some everyday burden or even some larger tragedy will inevitably darken the scene. Felt happiness is fragile and easily eclipsed. But, like the sun, real happiness can survive even through the storms.

Indeed, if one gives the imaginary person in the street a little more chance for reflection, they will nearly always come to see that happiness is something that lies deeper than today's particular tone. It can be compared to the flow of a river or a stream. When a strong wind comes, the surface of the water will be choppy and disturbed, and yet underneath the deeper waters flow calmly towards the sea. In something of the same way, the flow of a person's happiness can become troubled on the surface, because of some minor storm, but that is not the whole story of their search for happiness. There are other levels, deeper and steadier and more resistant to the passing winds.

> A person always experiences more through the fundamental living of life than he or she knows through self-reflection. The personal history of the experience of the self is the personal history of the experience of God.
> Karl Rahner (German theologian)

> Ask yourself whether you are happy and you cease to be so.
> John Stuart Mill (Nineteenth century English philosopher)

There is then a danger of an inadequate approach to the topic of happiness in everyday life. First impressions and first responses are not necessarily accurate guides. There exists a rich and profound hunger in everyone's life. It is acted out within the fragility of each day. It is inevitably influenced by random events. For many people it is more often a matter of the basic flow of a life than something understood or worked out with the mind. Above all it is not to be identified with unpredictable and changing situations. Therefore happiness is something more resilient than the flux of moods, and this is something that people know intuitively even though they may seldom reflect on it or put it into words.

Larger desires

Even on a humanist level, it is important to help people to recognise the existence of this rich desire within them. Later on this book will explore the evangelisation of this desire. For the moment the purpose is to approach the topic with a certain reverence for its mysterious depth. Happiness is not a superficial matter, even if it is all too often approached in these terms. It is a human experience that is subject to many distortions or reductions. People's ideals can fall victim to the version of happiness in the culture around that sees it simplistically in terms of externals. But if the suggestions here are valid, people are never truly satisfied with this restricted agenda of happiness. Their hearts are bigger than this. Intuitively they are aware of larger desires. Even if the experience of each day is changeable and vulnerable, there exists a stronger hope that can guide each life, and it is a vital service to anyone to help them discover that natural longing for happiness within each person.

2

CONVERGING LIGHTS ON HAPPINESS

The whole aim of humanity is to be happy. Finding happiness as one should is the source of every good. And the source of every evil is to find it where one should not.

Bossuet (Seventeenth century French bishop)

All people seek to be happy. This has no exceptions. Even though they use different means, they all aspire to this goal. It is the driving force of all the actions of every person, even of those who hang themselves.

Pascal (Seventeenth century French thinker)

As the two opening quotations suggest, what has never been doubted is that the desire for happiness is something universal and basic in humanity. This ever-present longing expresses itself in countless ways – in popular proverbs as well as in the labour of philosophers, in works of art or literature as well as in state legislation, at the core of religions and of family life.

It is hardly surprising that down through the ages people have tried to pin-point the nature of happiness. What really makes a person happy? Are some people more lucky than others in this respect? If so, is it just a question of chance? Or is there something more fundamental at stake? An assumption behind the inquiry was that the topic of happiness is central to culture and that any light on this issue would be of immense benefit to the struggles of humanity for meaning. In reflecting on the search for happiness one touches one of the most crucial of humanist and, indeed, of spiritual questions. Happiness is a deep human reality, but in what exactly does it consist? On that last question there is no clear consensus but one can at least mention some of the elements that might point towards a answer.

It may help to start from the personal: instead of asking what is happiness in the abstract, one can inquire into why people describe themselves as happy. In this respect, it is reported that one North American research project interviewed a hundred contented people.

The hope was to discover a common denominator. Interestingly, the first result was negative: happiness did not necessarily have anything to do with levels of wealth or even of education. At one point the researchers found that well over half of their happy hundred – about 70% in fact – came from small towns. But, although this might be significant, it proved not to be the key they were seeking. Eventually the researchers were forced to coin a word to describe what they found in all of their happy people: each of them was a "goodfinder" in the sense of having an ability to see good in everything and in everyone.

Happiness as by-product

> A goodfinder is one who looks for and finds what is good in him or herself, in others, and in all the situations of life. If we set ourselves to find evil, there is plenty of it to be discovered. On the other hand, if we seek to find goodness, there is also much goodness waiting for our discovery.
>
> John Powell (American writer)

> Two men looked out from prison bars
> One saw mud and one saw stars.
>
> Verse proverb

Obviously such a positive attitude is a great blessing and is usually the by-product of happy experiences in family, in upbringing, and most of all in the evolving disposition of heart that exists in every person. It is close to what some theologians have called a "fundamental option". Something of the same idea has been captured in more popular American language by claiming that happiness is "an inside job". Both expressions put the emphasis on happiness not as an accident but rather as the outcome of human freedom and

22

choice. As such, there is even a sense in which people are responsible for their own happiness, and for protecting it against being undermined.

Even already three converging factors in happiness have appeared: it is a gift and a disposition and an option. This ability to see good is learned from others, and in particular from the love of others – therefore a gift. It builds up as an attitude that shapes a person's responses to reality – therefore a disposition. Gradually it comes to be a chosen attitude, a way of responding to experience – therefore an option.

This rather optimistic analysis needs qualification. Clearly some people have more fortunate life situations than others, not only in matters of external comfort, but in the deeper influences of a loving home or a secure environment. If happiness is something learned, it is an easier lesson for some than for others. There are psychological factors in everyone's upbringing that can help or hinder the blossoming of a happy disposition later in life. Where someone is constantly blamed, they can develop a poor level of self-esteem and may well need contrary experiences of self-worth in order to see their own potential and actual goodness. Indeed it is striking that the biblical command to "love one's neighbour as oneself" implies that genuine self-love lies at the root of being able to love others.

Fruit of self-giving

> The reason why all mankind do not find happiness, when they are so anxious for it, is that they are seeking it. If they would seek the glory of God, and the good of the universe as their supreme end, **it** would pursue them.
>
> Charles Finney (Nineteenth century American preacher)

> Nobody has true joy unless he or she lives in love.
>
> St Thomas Aquinas

There is a traditional metaphor that happiness is like a butterfly: if you pursue it, it will escape you, but if you stay quiet it will come near. In other words, happiness is not the *direct* object of human desire, or rather if it is made so, it becomes self-defeating. Happiness is a state of mind, a condition of harmony, and as such it is nearly always the by-product of a way of life rather than a target in itself. One could list many possible marks of the happy life, or rather of the life that bears fruit in a sense of happiness. Some have already been touched upon, or at least implied in what has been said so far: self-acceptance, gratitude, the gift of seeing good in everything, growing in trust in spite of the handicaps of past experience, living from responsibility and choice. But, as St Paul might say, one gift is the greatest: the surest road to happiness is to live with generosity and self-giving love.

It is worth adding at this stage that although many of these elements of happiness might seem to echo Christian values, in fact they are shared with non-believers. Many of them, as will be seen, were present even in a pre-Christian thinker like Aristotle. It is true that Christian revelation casts new light and gives new focus and strength for this perennial quest. But the search for happiness belongs to all of humanity, believer or non-believer alike, and similarly, many of the basics of happiness are common to all people of good will.

3

HAPPINESS IN THE FACE OF SUFFERING

> To create something means being rescued from the darkness of the individual self. No matter what price of suffering has to be paid, I call that a state of happiness.
>
> Pierre Emmanuel (French poet)

> You have to have courage to be happy.
>
> Joseph Joubert (Nineteenth century French writer)

Five days before he died in 1963, Pope John XXIII sent a letter to a young girl in Genoa called Rosanna Benzi. Some two years previously, at the age of thirteen, she had been struck down by poliomyelitis and was living in an iron lung. The Pope wrote to thank her for her will to live, and indeed Rosanna continued to demonstrate that same courage and cheerfulness until she died in February 1991 at the age of forty-two. Through the twenty-nine years during which she lived in the iron lung, she made a name for herself as a person of humanity and energy, even founding and editing a magazine for handicapped people.

Rosanna Benzi is a proof of something crucial to all these reflections on happiness: it has already become clear that there is an element of choice within happiness and this is all the more evident when confronted with tragedy or suffering. In such a situation happiness involves an option lived against all the odds. So the outer situation is not necessarily the determining factor in whether someone's life is truly happy or not. On a personal level happiness stems from the mysterious realm of human freedom. Or, as St John of the Cross once said, what matters is not what happens but how one responds to what happens.

To recall such a victory over tragedy is to protect ourselves from thinking of happiness as something cheap or easy. Indeed even in the long Western tradition of tragic drama, it is striking that a similar pattern recurs: again and again a hero or heroine is confronted with darkness but even though their outer journey is towards death, something of a triumph of the spirit is often present in the final stage of the play. One has only to think of the mood evoked towards the close of Shakespeare's *King Lear* to realise that something of Christian transcendence is at work: people rise above their normal selves. The old king and his daughter Cordelia enter into a stage of perception beyond suffering. What is being dramatised is the human capacity not to surrender to despair, the strength to opt for an attitude that does not escape pain but transcends it spiritually.

Few people, however, are asked to face the burdens of heavy handicap like Rosanna Benzi, or the totality of defeat like King Lear. Rather, these extraordinary figures are symbols of a human capacity for happiness in spite of the burdens of existence. Every life has its share of pain and anxiety. No life is without darkness and shadow. Therefore whatever one means by happiness must be strong enough to embrace these inevitable struggles and sufferings.

Option of transcendence

It gradually becomes clear that this demanding kind of happiness needs an option of self-transcendence so that people begin to live no longer with themselves at the centre: it entails a personal Copernican revolution. When this happens, happiness comes about as the by-product of a generous way of living, and not a direct goal in itself. Confronted with suffering, it becomes even clearer that happiness stems from a commitment to go beyond egoism and to reach out beyond the isolated self to the calls and cries of others. Once again, as already mentioned, happiness is the fruit of an option to live lovingly, and this commitment is all the more remarkable in a situation of suffering. To say this is very close to the spirit of the gospels, but for the moment it is enough to describe happiness in human terms, "from below" so to speak.

Most people are about as happy as they choose to be.
Abraham Lincoln

Happiness is a choice. Many people do choose it. But fail to attain it because they seek happiness in the wrong way.
Ismael Maningas (Philippine academic)

Provided it is alive, faith allows the Christian to integrate even suffering, to accept it in a positive way without needing to repress anything and without retreating to resignation.
Vjekoslav Bajsic (Croatian theologian)

In ordinary existence, the danger is that happiness can sink into the trivial, that the heart can rest content with the second-rate, and above all that the invitation to grow in options of self-giving can be avoided. But life seldom allows a person to stay asleep in this way. Sooner or later something will jolt the drifter out of his or her slumber. What are these moments of awakening? The American novelist Saul Bellow has expressed it wittily through the main character in *The Adventures of Augie March:* there are, he says, two great awakeners of the spirit from its sleep, love and suffering. And he adds: love can do it, but suffering is sure.

Happiness, in normal experience and understanding, can be described as a convergence of several factors: a gift from family circumstances, a disposition that grows with time, a decision for generosity, a state of harmony within the person. Here the additional insight is that it is born of life-decisions for self-transcendence. Bellow's light on this process would suggest that certain privileged moments in life – or in religious terms, moments of grace – arise mainly through two kinds of experience. Whenever a person runs into love, the heart awakens from the superficial, but even more infallibly, whenever a person runs into tragedy and manages to find the courage to respond with wisdom, the door is open to a different dimension of happiness. Thus happiness is rooted in a response to life that goes beyond the ego. The wisdom of this happiness is a costly one. And once again one is close to the gospels with their paradoxical promises that whoever loses their life will find it. To arrive at a happiness worthy of the human heart will usually involve a letting-go of more superficial hopes and desires, and this letting-go is often the fruit of some struggle with either love or suffering.

> The search for happiness inevitably entails a struggle for self-transcendence.
>
> Cardinal Silvano Piovanelli (Archbishop of Florence)

> If you want to be happy, then you must forget about being happy. Only *meaning* gives purpose to life and to be happy, one must seek that meaning in some cause greater than one's own selfish desire to be happy.
>
> Richard Kroph (American theologian)

Awakened by the needs of others

So far these pages have been considering only those occasions of life when some personal conflict can be the source of surprising strength and ultimately an opening into a deeper kind of happiness. It has been seen that happiness and struggle are not necessarily enemies, and that human beings are capable of rising to heights of generosity precisely when faced with some shock to their previous securities. But there is another possibility that points in the same direction: the cry of the world's pain can also be an awakener of the spirit towards a generosity characterised by a happiness much deeper than that born from "corn and new wine".

Perhaps one could describe this avenue to happiness as involving "a Moses moment". One recalls the time when Moses awoke to his calling through hearing the cry of his own suffering people. Indeed, in his message for the beginning of Lent in 1991, Pope John Paul II encouraged as a preparation for the "joy of Easter" that people become aware of "the heart-rending misery that afflicts so many parts of the world", and then overcome indifference through practical love and solidarity.

This is another version of an option for happiness that can confront tragedy and enter the struggle against it. In many parts of the world faith comes alive as a source of happiness when young people give themselves to voluntary service, especially for the most wounded in our society. Far from giving rise to depression, the contact with suffering can become yet another birthplace of that self-transcendence which is *the* basis of happiness.

Contrary to what might be expected, happiness is neither a matter of luck, nor of avoiding pain. In English the very term "happiness" is connected with "hap", in the sense of chance or good fortune. But in reality what one discovers to be true happiness is not so fortuitous: it is rooted in a free choice to live generously. Even if, in ordinary usage, the idea of happiness can conjure up a superficial or transitory satisfaction, there is much more at stake than this level of contentment. The happiness explored here is capable of embracing the darker side of existence and of responding with compassion and courage.

4

THREE PHILOSOPHERS: ARISTOTLE, AQUINAS, JULIAN MARIAS

Happiness is not a matter of luck. It has to be created.
André Comte-Sponville (French philosopher)

But if we are talking of perfect happiness, which awaits us in the homeland, then mankind will have the plenitude of its fulfilment in God.
St Thomas Aquinas

To complete the exploration of the many ways in which happiness is discovered by different people, one can call on the evidence of two other groups of people – philosophers and saints. The philosophers to be looked at will be Aristotle, St Thomas Aquinas and Julián Marías. Then, in the following chapter, the saints in question will be St Francis of Assisi, St Ignatius Loyola and St John of the Cross.

Julián Marías, the Spanish philosopher, published *La felicidad humana* in 1987. Less than six months later he found himself writing a new preface to a second edition: the theme of happiness had proved so popular that the first edition sold out within a short time. This simple fact shows how this ancient theme still strikes many chords and that, if properly communicated, it can prove a live question for people today. In the words of Marías, happiness is a strictly personal issue that needs to be approached on the level of experience: "seldom do we bother to inquire into our own experience; we seek for happiness without paying much attention to it".

It is typical of the contemporary thinker to start from lived experience – as has been done in these pages so far – but older schools of thought approached the issue in an interestingly different way. Their emphasis was more objective and focused on an inquiry into the overall purpose of life. Perhaps both approaches are needed. Happiness is, as Marías rightly insists, an essentially personal issue. But it also involves larger horizons of meaning: a philosophy of happiness that stays within the subjective will lack foundations and ultimately will not do justice to the range of human desire.

Focus on the future

The approach adopted by Marías is attractive in many respects, perhaps especially because of his insistence on the dramatic quality in the human experience of happiness. A key element for him – and one that has not been mentioned in any detail here so far – is that happiness involves a thrust into the future. As such it is a form of hope, always anticipating a greater fulfilment to come. Thus the achievement of happiness in this life remains insecure, never more than partial and always marked by incompletion. For Marías happiness is characterised by desire or longing rather than by achieved satisfaction. Indeed he remarks that success in happiness can be dangerous: one has never really arrived, because there is always more.

> *Boswell*: Sir, you observed one day that a man is never happy for the present, but when he is drunk. Will you not add, or when driving rapidly in a post-chaise?
> *Johnson*: No. Sir, you are driving rapidly from something or to something.
> Samuel Johnson (Eighteenth century English writer)

> So many people in our time identify happiness with other things. Happiness is life itself, when it attains its fullness.
> Julián Marías (Spanish philosopher)

This Spanish study warns its readers not to confuse happiness with either its causes or its effects. It can originate from concrete circumstances of life but these are not to be identified with happiness. It can be accompanied by pleasure or by various psychological states of harmony, but these are not the core of happiness. It is something more profound and dynamic and its two great enemies are fear and lack of imagination.

There are many paradoxical truths concerning happiness. It can be fleeting in terms of intensity and yet steady and rooted in a person's life: "I can be settled in happiness even though I know it will not last". Or again, it is an active orientation towards the future and yet it is anchored in the present. It can stem from one dimension of life, such as family love, and yet it will spread out, with a radiation effect, to influence all of a person's activity. Its strength can even embrace situations of outer pain or objective unhappiness such as war or imprisonment. A person can be "happy in spite of everything".

A constant drama

What Marías brings out eloquently is that although it might be easy to define happiness in various ideal and abstract ways, in the actual flow of life it is always changing and always under threat. And yet it can remain a steady thread right through a person's life. In his view it is part of a constant struggle for fullness of life, and this adventure gathers each life into a unity or biography. By approaching the issue experientially and metaphysically, Marías is able to highlight three complementary aspects of happiness. It is an adventure of risk and of vulnerability. It is an anchor holding a person's life together. It is an invitation of fidelity to one's own depths of desire.

In contrast with this elevated view of happiness, unfortunately many people live beneath their level of possibility and therefore miss the call that is written into their humanity. This powerful synthesis points also to fundamentally Christian horizons. Marías remarks that two keystones were unavailable to pagan philosophers: a sense of the ultimate goal of existence and the primacy of love.

Although the search for happiness was seen in antiquity as a key task for philosophy, even to pose the question nowadays risks seeming individualist. Utilitarianism accepts the modern reduction of happiness to pleasure as experienced.

Anton Stres (Slovenian philosopher)

Our biggest obstacle to believing in God is our innate distrust of happiness. This is a disbelief in our own goodness.

Sebastian Moore (English Benedictine theologian)

In *Centesimus annus* Pope John Paul II diagnoses a certain cultural poverty in a merely secular approach to life: he speaks of this stance as suffering from a "desire to possess things rather than to relate them to the truth, and lacking that disinterested, unselfish and aesthetic attitude that is born of wonder in the presence of being" (37). This critique would delight Aristotle, because he too insisted on linking his discussion of happiness to such fundamentals as human rationality, truth and, ultimately, the capacity for contemplative wonder.

The classical viewpoint
In the history of pondering the question of happiness, the achievement of Aristotle represents an early peak of insight and wisdom that has never become irrelevant. Christian thought modified and expanded his basic ideas in this respect, but his synthesis remains as valid now as in his own day. Indeed his emphasis on a non-subjectivist and non-utilitarian version of happiness offers a perfect antidote to the immanentist notions prevalent in modern times.

Happiness is subjective. Only the study of subjectivity can point us towards it.

Dominique Laplane (French writer)

The highest good is a soul that despises things of chance and takes pleasure in virtue.

Seneca

The modest aim here is to gather some of the freshness and clarity of Aristotle's understanding of happiness. The assumption behind his *Nicomachean Ethics* is that everything has a purpose and in this light he sees happiness as the goal of all human energies. But Aristotle is also down-to-earth and realistic in insisting that happiness is only possible if certain basic conditions are fulfilled. For instance, a person will need some material security: without food and shelter the desire for happiness will be displaced onto such essentials. Or again, people will need to have reached a certain psychological and moral maturity: without this they will tend to identify happiness with immediate satisfactions.

In tune with reason

The core of Aristotle's understanding of happiness is that it involves the realisation of a person's rational nature. His most famous statement in this regard is that happiness consists in a "virtuous activity of the soul". In other words happiness is the fruit of integrated living where human freedom is guided by reason and where people follow a path of objective moral goodness.

With his typical realism Aristotle recognised that to live in tune with reason will always entail struggle. "Prudence" was the name he gave to the virtue which is able to mediate between reason and affectivity in this regard. Finally, in an extraordinary insight for a pagan philosopher, Aristotle goes on to say that a person will not live according to this high standard simply out of human resources but "in so far as there is something divine within".

In short, Aristotle was strikingly positive about the human potential for happiness: in his view it is normal to seek happiness and ideally it should be normal for each person to reach a certain happiness, however limited by circumstances and by the degree to which a person uses his or her freedom wisely. Underlying his understanding of happiness is a metaphysical position of the goodness of being. Hence it is only through acting in harmony with one's full humanity that a person will be truly happy. Indeed the entire Aristotelian approach to moral philosophy has as its foundation the drive of each person towards happiness, and human beings were meant for higher reaches of happiness, well beyond the simple level of sense pleasures. But Aristotle goes even further: for him the deepest form of happiness comes from a contemplative activity that suggests at least a sharing in the happiness of God.

> The story of the thief on the cross is unintelligible in Aristotelian terms.
>
> Alasdair MacIntyre (Scottish philosopher)

> For the Angelic Doctor the question of happiness is not abstract nor on a purely speculative level: it stems directly from experience, or more precisely from Christian experience as containing and deepening human experience.
>
> Servais Pinckaers (Dominican theologian)

No wonder that a millennium and a half later St Thomas Aquinas admired Aristotle so much and especially concerning this topic of happiness! In fact Aquinas gives exceptional prominence to this theme in the general structure of his thought, and like Aristotle he understands it in terms of a dynamism of human activity towards a supreme goal. Happiness, in his view, constitutes the foundation-stone of morality because it is the ultimate purpose of all human existence. Thus he builds on the Aristotelian tradition but gathers into it many lights from such Christian thinkers as St Augustine or Boethius. Predictably, it is over the promise of eternal happiness with God that Aquinas departs most radically from Aristotle's treatment. As St Thomas put it on several occasions, Aristotle dealt with "imperfect happiness, reachable in this present life". While this is an important issue for Aquinas also, his real emphasis falls on the more perfect happiness beyond this world. Thus the Thomist standpoint builds both on reason and on revelation.

From Augustine to Aquinas
A few words of comparison with St Augustine may help towards appreciating the particular approach of St Thomas to the theme of happiness. Augustine was more introspective and less systematic

in his thought. For him also the question of desire for fulfilment was utterly central, as evidenced even in the most famous sentence on the first page of his *Confessions:* "You have made us for yourself and our hearts are restless until they find their rest in you". The story that Augustine tells of his own life is one of a long and desperate search for happiness in false directions. In all this wandering he only experienced what he called "a fugitive's freedom". Thus the trigger for his discovery of faith lay, one might say, in the unhappiness of his search for happiness. His ultimate conversion was intimately linked with a surrender to another happiness – as a gift of God and as recognised only in the light of love: "If we love, we see".

St Augustine's dramatic journey towards the truth was a journey out of false and into true happiness. At its core was deep desire. But for many years that desire was focused on secondaries. In his own eloquent words, he remained "in love with loving" and therefore missed recognising the presence of the Lover. In short, the Augustinian approach to happiness is psychological, inductive, and rooted in the intensity of his spiritual biography. The Thomist approach is much more ordered and deductive. He starts by asking what is the ultimate goal of life. He answers in terms of happiness both as object and as act. Above all, the principal form of happiness that he has in mind is the fullness of life and enjoyment with God. This happiness is contemplative rather than speculative, a vision of truth for the mind rather than simply the object of desire, and it is the highest good for humankind.

Sharing in God's happiness
This high interpretation of happiness can appear distant and abstract today. Far from it. For St Thomas the key to understanding happiness comes from seeing it as sharing in the happiness of God, and so the whole topic becomes deeply personal for him. Even in what he calls the imperfect happiness of this world, Aquinas sees "a certain participation" in the fullness that is yet to come. Thus he is positive about the many forms of enjoyment that accompany happiness in this life. They do not exhaust the meaning

of happiness – because its fullness comes only with the vision of God's love in eternity – but ordinary experiences of happiness are like mirrors of that future fullness.

Moreover, Aquinas insists on linking happiness with the good deeds performed in this life. He agrees with Aristotle that the exercise of virtue is the principal road to happiness here but of course he sees this also in terms of the crowning of goodness through the gift of eternal life. For him, however, there is only one happiness, with different faces. There is a unity rather than a dichotomy between the flow of happiness in this life and in eternity. Union with God through enjoyment of the truth is the ultimate happiness but that vision is the fulfilment of the love or "virtue" lived out in this life. This fullness of happiness for Aquinas involves the convergence of three elements: a vision, a presence, and an enjoyment of quiet love. This rich synthesis was marvellously expressed by Dante as follows:

> Luce intellettual, piena d'amore
> amor di vero ben, pien di letizia
> letizia che trascende ogni dolzore.
>
> *Paradiso*, xxx, 40-42

> [Light for the mind, filled with love,
> love of the true good, filled with delight,
> a delight outrunning all other sweetness.]

5

THREE SAINTS: FRANCIS OF ASSISI, JOHN OF THE CROSS, IGNATIUS LOYOLA

There is only one way of being happy: not to be ignorant of suffering and not to run away from it, but to accept the transfiguration it brings.

Henri de Lubac (French theologian and Cardinal)

Only the saints are truly happy.

Léon Bloy (French writer)

Ignatius

The experience of three rather different saints offers another perspective on happiness. Even though he is not the first historically, St Ignatius' self-discovery about happiness is something that can help ordinary people, even non-believers, in searching for criteria of genuine happiness in their own experience.

The relevant moment for St Ignatius is what he himself described as his "first ever insight into things of a spiritual kind". Its context was the time of his convalescence after he had nearly died of battle wounds and the crude surgery of the sixteenth century. It is a well-known story that while waiting to recover he asked for some reading material. He wanted some of the popular romances of the day that he had been addicted to as a courtier, but his pious sister-in-law gave him some lives of the saints and a book about Christ. Out of boredom he actually read them and, being both an imaginative and a methodical man, he began to divide his day into different periods – fantasising about returning to his old life as a courtier or alternatively fantasising about what it would be like to become a saint like Dominic or Francis. The contrast of these two daydreams was to be the source of his conversion, and his resultant self-discovery focused on the question of happiness or consolation.

Discerning true from false
In his autobiography Ignatius tells how both subjects gave him equal absorption and pleasure at the time, but when he left these imaginings aside, he noticed a difference in his mood afterwards. "He understood from experience that one subject of thought left him dejection, while the other left him joy." He had stumbled onto a crucial distinction, however simple, and one which was to become the foundation for discerning between true and false consolation or happiness. Does the sense of joy remain? Does it last and bear fruit in love? If so, it can be trusted to be from the "good spirit". This became the source of the Ignatian contribution to the tradition of discernment of spirits, and it can be of relevance in helping people distinguish true from false happiness, starting from their own experience.

Genuine happiness will not be short-lived – it will be strong enough to bear lasting fruit. This was a characteristic of the experience of Rosanna Benzi, evoked some pages back. The Ignatian light is that it is possible to become aware of contrasting spiritual moods within oneself and to discern what is from God in terms of its fruits. Happiness is born from a continual conflict between true and false, and the genuine article is known by its capacity to endure and to grow in love. What leads towards self-giving or self-transcendence is recognisable because it brings a harmony or peace that lasts. Thus, within one's own experience of the flux of happiness it is possible to discern the superficial from the deep, the transitory from the lasting. It is possible to learn what is truly in tune with the hopes of one's heart. This moment from the life of St Ignatius suggests a practical way of recognising true happiness: people are normally meant to experience consolation whenever they are living fully and generously.

John of the Cross

The most frequent accusation against Christian happiness is that it relegates everything to another life. However, John of

the Cross speaks more about happiness in this life than in
the next.

Ismael Bengoechea (Spanish Carmelite writer)

With St John of the Cross one will find experiences of fullness
expressed in a more dramatic and powerful way. From his different spirituality comes a different light on happiness: even in this
life people can, in a sense, know the joy of encountering God. In
spite of all his emphasis on the dark night and on the cost of the
many purifications of the human spirit in prayer, St John is one
who both witnesses to and celebrates another dimension of potential happiness in human experience.

Throughout his writings one can find a huge variety of ways in
which he evokes this extraordinary happiness of a spiritual kind.
The joy that he speaks of is certainly not cheap and may in practice be rare. But St John of the Cross is a constant invitation to
people to undertake that deeper journey into a more fulfilling happiness. As Pope John Paul II said, on the fourth centenary of the
saint's death, he offers an example of faith developing "in its contemplative dimension. The Christian must encounter God in mystery". This master of prayer leads people beyond dependence "on
pleasant or unpleasant feelings" to being "led by faith and by
love".

Once again one can notice the contrast between superficial and
genuine levels of happiness. Within the eloquent and poetic writings of St John of the Cross, it is also striking to what extent he
uses the language of human pleasures and joys to evoke happiness
of a mystical kind. Although he insists that the encounter with God
is such a "delicate and deep delight that there is no way to describe
it in mortal language", in fact he constantly uses images drawn
from the enjoyment of the senses, or from the poetry of human
love, to evoke this happiness indirectly. "Happy the life, happy the
state, and happy the soul that reaches this point where everything
is the essence of love and of gift and of the delight of nuptials".

This great poet and mystic envisages a deep, if often neglected,
capacity for happiness in everyone. All that is needed is freedom

from the blockages, and certainly that process of liberation is costly. But when the spirit is set free, an adventure of joy awaits, even if it continues always in tension with darkness. "Your joy is inside you", says St John and his whole work gives witness to that dimension of happiness as lived. For him the "sweetness and delights of love" are available within the soul and therefore "it cannot be heavy or pained, because this [happiness through love] is the goal of all its troubles and the root of all its good". For St John of the Cross within each person is a wavelength of love and of reaching out to love, and this is the foundation of his powerful presentation of happiness.

Francis

The saint universally famous for his spirit of celebration and of happiness is undoubtedly Francis of Assisi. What was at the heart of his happiness? What constituted for him the pinnacle of happiness in this world? In some ways his answer is both surprising and challenging. It is found in a marvellous chapter of his *Fioretti* in which he captures, with the charm of a little story, what for him would be perfect joy.

One day, while out walking with Brother Leo, St Francis began to speak, at intervals along the road, of the many good qualities that he noticed in his friars and that gave him happiness. But to each one of them, except the last, he added, "write down that this is not perfect joy". Thus he mentioned such high gifts as being examples of holiness, or being able to heal the blind or even to raise the dead. A little later he adds gifts of languages or of prophecy, or knowledge of all the secrets of the earth. But these, he says, would not be perfect joy. Eventually, as if his patience is at an end, Brother Leo asks, "Tell me, in the name of God, wherein lies perfect joy?"

By way of climax and answer St Francis asks him to imagine arriving home to the community, wet and tired and hungry, but the porter does not believe that they are two of the brothers, calls them beggars and liars and leaves them outside for the night in the cold. "Then if we bear with patience the wrong done with such cruelty and insults – bear it with calmness and without complaint, humbly and charitably believing that the porter really thinks so, God having inspired him to speak against us – O Brother Leo, write down that in this is perfect joy".

Even though the text does not mention it explicitly, at the heart of St Francis' "perfect joy" is the sense of sharing the lot of Christ. The imitation of Christ involves, as St Paul had expressed it, knowing "the power of his resurrection and sharing his sufferings" (Ph 3:10). Such a source of joy underlies the vision of St Francis. His is a happiness suffused and inspired with the spirit of the Beatitudes.

Happiness as God's gift

Happiness is a rich and multi-faceted reality. St Ignatius Loyola stressed the ordinary blessings of God's consolation as discerned in everyday experience. St John of the Cross explored the more extraordinary heights and depths of spiritual bliss where a person is overwhelmed by the love of God. St Francis of Assisi, as well as celebrating the beauty of creation, invites us to realise the special joy involved in sharing the heart of Christ, even to the point of suffering like him. All three deal with the variety of happiness as God's gift. All three celebrate the potential freedom of spirit that answers, in exceptional ways, the human hunger for happiness.

Hearing the saints in this way is like listening to the apostle John: "There are several things I have to tell you, but I have thought it best not to trust them to paper and ink. I hope instead to visit you and talk to you personally so that our joy may be complete" (2 Jn 12-13).

Part Two

HAPPINESS IN CONTEMPORARY CULTURE

6

A GLANCE AT RECENT HISTORY

Happiness is a new idea in Europe.
Saint-Just (French revolutionary)

Of all political ideals, that of making people happy is the most dangerous.
Karl Popper (Austrian philosopher)

The contrast of these two quotations offers a quick summary of the rise and fall of a particular political hope within the last few centuries. It has been a time when the question of happiness entered the vocabulary of politics in many different ways and was often written into national constitutions as a principal goal for citizens.

Political experiments

The famous claim of Saint-Just leaves itself open to attack as simply untrue: in fact happiness had been the subject of study in Europe for centuries and was examined in depth in ancient and medieval times as something central to the very purpose of human life. However, the celebrated partisan of the French Revolution would surely defend himself by saying that the happiness he had in mind was new in two ways: it was intended for everyone and it would be fostered by new political structures of democracy. A new order would open the door to unprecedented possibilities for the whole people. Such was the revolutionary hope that was born with the Enlightenment and gave rise to the upheavals of the late eighteenth century in Europe and elsewhere.

This happiness was envisaged as the product of a new politics. That was a key element of its newness as an idea. Moreover, this happiness could claim newness in four other significant ways. It would focus on the social rather than on the personal. It would be aided by an economics of industrial production, entailing new possibilities of wealth for the masses. This would permit unheard-of availability of education for everyone with a resultant increase in human awareness and happiness. And this whole process would be radically secular, rejecting all religious interpretations of happiness as illusory and alienating.

From Utopia of happiness to reign of terror

The greater the hope, the deeper was the disillusion, and it was one of tragic dimensions. The first fruit of the revolutionary Utopia of happiness for all was a disaster for many. One need only think of the time of terror after 1792, of the deportations into inhuman conditions, of the flight abroad of tens of thousands of people, and of the mass executions. And once this bloody wave of revolution was over, what remained of the humanistic hopes of Saint-Just?

Contrary to what was envisaged by those false political ideals, what in fact emerged was a new and large European middle class, interested mainly in a happiness of domestic tranquillity and of increasing comfort of life. With surprising rapidity the fire of revolution gave way to the fire in the sitting-room as a symbol of happiness. A new society was born but its horizons quickly narrowed into preservation of the status quo. The great theme of happiness that had occupied philosophers through the centuries shrank into the narrow interests typical of the *nouveau riche*. Novelists as varied as Balzac or Dickens specialised in exposing the identification of happiness with possessions. And at the same time a gradual secularisation was gnawing away at European consciousness: for many of the new dominant class religion was marginalised into being a pleasant icing on the cake of comfort, a way of gesturing from time to time towards the God who made their satisfactions possible.

> The greatest happiness of the greatest number is the foundation of morals and legislation.
> Jeremy Bentham (Nineteenth century British philosopher)

Meanwhile a more militant version of political happiness was being prepared. The social and industrial revolutions that brought new comfort to an emerging middle class in fact left the mass of people in more degrading situations than before. Previously the majority of people had lived in rural situations of struggling poverty but often this peasant life had great dignity and enjoyed the blessings of genuine community and of an inherited Christian faith. Quite suddenly thousands found themselves having to leave the land and move to the new cities. The magnet drawing them was the mere possibility of more work and more money – as it is again today in many a third-world situation of similarly rampant urbanisation. Thus it was that around 1840 England became the first country in world history to have a majority of its population living in urban situations.

This unprecedented fact was soon to be echoed in other countries, and everywhere it changed the face of human society and the language of human hopes. The Christian Church had long been rooted in the country or in smaller town situations. In this new setting of urban living, the absence of community, the inevitable anonymity and the tendency to relativise moral values, all contributed to a major crisis of faith itself. Happiness was also in crisis. On the one hand it was increasingly identified with material success and satisfactions. On the other hand new forms of injustice and unhappiness were born in the crowded cities and in the unhealthy factories where even children worked.

The anthropological disaster of Marxism

A society based on pure competition cannot survive. . . Many dictatorships have been born from the false conviction that society could be scientifically explained and controlled.

Agnes Heller (Hungarian philosopher)

This urban and industrial world was the seedbed for the whole Marxist critique of the existing order and for his proposed revolution. His new and false idea of happiness was to be more systematically pursued than that of Saint-Just and became the greatest anthropological catastrophe ever for millions of people. It was this Marxist version of controlled and materialist happiness that Karl Popper had in mind in the second of the two quotations that began this chapter. The huge tragedy of this period of history is now coming to its close. Marxism thought of itself as a scientific project that could offer material happiness to entire populations. But it has failed miserably, both on the level of human rights and on the level of economic achievement, and this only serves to show how an anthropological error, offering a one-sided answer to social unhappiness, only produces new versions of unhappiness on a global and world level.

Just as the dream of happiness, born from the Enlightenment thinking of Saint-Just, gave rise to the blood-letting and tragedy of the French Revolution two centuries ago, so too the atheist ideology of marxism, imposed in the name of a mistaken political goal, instead of making the masses happy and liberating them from the so-called alienation of religion, produced the most enormous totalitarian system in the history of humanity. Once it reduced the human person to the merely material and economic dimension, it resulted in an inhuman economics and politics. This was the root cause of its inevitable failure.

This was rightly emphasised by the Synod of European Bishops: the collapse of communism puts in question the whole thrust of that cultural and socio-political humanism in Europe which has been marked with atheism. The facts show, and not only in the example of marxism, that as a matter of principle it is not possible to divorce the cause of God from the cause of humanity. There can never be a genuine human happiness, for people or for societies, apart from the truth about humanity as created in the image and likeness of God.

Orwell and Huxley

The social problem of today is the inability to love or suffer, an inability to accept pain . . . A culture that rejects unhappi-

ness becomes pathological, and in fact ours is a society without goals and incapable of big desires.
Vera Slepoj (Italian psychologist)

There is an obsessive character to the search for happiness in our society. Boredom is seen as a great threat. People are often gratified, never satisfied.
Archbishop Eric D'Arcy (Australia)

Two contrasting novels of modern English literature have often been used to summarise a difference between two forms of social oppression in today's world. George Orwell's *Nineteen Eighty-Four* is looked on as a classic exposure of military and psychological forms of totalitarianism in the state. It can be seen as echoing in many ways the crudest excesses of communism as a system of control through terror and force. By comparison Aldous Huxley's earlier *Brave New World* depicted a very different undermining of human values through a system of imposed hedonism. Huxley was thinking rather of capitalist versions of paradise and in satiric fashion simply magnified the world of consumerism into a fantasy of a situation where people would "love their servitude". His picture is of a world where struggle is unknown, where solitude is sickness, where religious sentiment is superfluous, and where everyone is pleasantly drugged into conformity. It is highly significant that Bernard, the rebel of the book, voices his rejection of such triviality in these words: "I don't want comfort. I want God, I want poetry, I want real danger, I want freedom, I want goodness. I want sin . . . I'm claiming the right to be unhappy".

Happiness and freedom

The paradoxical truth underlying that last surprising word is that it is impossible to be genuinely happy, or to grow morally, without some struggle with unhappiness. The bland and painless life forced on people in *Brave New World* is a deliberately exaggerated picture of the surface pleasures promoted by the so-called Western or Americanised life-style. The main dehumanising effect of the hedonist paradise presented by Huxley is the killing of human freedom, and the result is a reduction of happiness from being rooted in choice to being simply a banal sequence of childish distractions.

> A radical dimension of lovelessness can be hidden by sustained superficiality and then the absence of fulfilment reveals itself in unrest, the absence of joy in the pursuit of fun, the absence of peace in disgust.
>
> Bernard Lonergan (Canadian theologian)

> Nowadays the right to happiness in the sense of welfare is a basic concept and characteristic of humanity.
>
> Bishop Anton Schlembach (Germany)

Unfortunately this fiction is not that far from reality in many people's lives today. Pope John Paul II offered a penetrating critique of consumerist culture in *Centesimus annus:* "Exploitation, at least in the forms analysed and described by Karl Marx, has been overcome in Western society. Alienation, however, has not been overcome as it exists in various forms of exploitation, when people use one another, and when they seek an ever more refined satisfaction of their individual and secondary needs, while ignoring the principal and authentic needs . . .The collapse of the Communist system in so many countries certainly removes an obstacle to facing these problems in an appropriate and realistic way, but it is not enough to bring about their solution" (41, 42).

Those statements present an eloquent analysis and judgement of the attractive but false happiness on offer in today's culture. They identify a moral tone for this contemporary moment in the history of happiness. They raise the question as to whether the more comfortable parts of our planet live a rather blinkered happiness – content with possessions and pleasures of a small kind, and therefore cut off from deeper sources of vision, and of authentic living of happiness.

The parable of the sower

> Distracted from distraction by distraction.
>
> T. S. Eliot

> An inquiry into literature would show how often happiness is dismissed or becomes an object of derision. One needs to remind our culture that we are made for happiness: that happiness is primary and that if unhappiness is deeply resented, it is because the depth of our spirit is inhabited by an instinct for happiness.
>
> Georges Cottier (Theologian of the Pontifical household)

There are many diverse situations today where this conflict of true and false happiness is being acted out. But the central drama is between the powerful images that keep people imprisoned in the superficial and the genuine hungers of the human heart. It is an ancient story. It is in many ways a rewriting in contemporary complexity of the conflict described by Jesus in the parable of the Sower. In the commentary on that parable offered in Matthew's gospel, the thorns that choke the growth of the seed are described as "the distractions of this world and the lure of wealth" (Mt 13:22).

That old temptation has simply found more sophisticated expression in the contemporary world. The plot is familiar but the technology of distraction is overwhelming in an unprecedented way. A new element that cuts across all differences in cultures and situations is the power of television in promoting false images of happiness. If sophisticated culture has often been dominated by images of pessimism, popular culture seems to be a supermarket of superficial optimism. Even a poor hut in a Latin American *barrio* is now likely to have its own television set. It is a symbol of a new era not only in communications but also in the history of happiness. Never before have so many people been so easily and quickly influenced by one source of values. Never before has there been such a bombardment of the human imagination with trivial but attractive portrayals of happiness.

Indeed, the battleground for values today is increasingly located in the world of images rather than in the world of pure ideas. And this is where many people have few defences, where their inherited faith is particularly vulnerable to assault. It is in this light that the conflict of images of happiness is seen to be of vital relevance for the communication of faith itself. Where the merely trivial occupies the heart, and does so through attractive images, this influences the possibility of that "hearing" from which faith comes. To adapt the metaphors of that parable again, the very ground into which the seed must be sown can be damaged or polluted. The propaganda of images can be much more destructive for faith than the older propaganda of militant atheism.

Once again the site of this struggle is happiness. The human heart intuitively seeks ways of happiness. If the roads to happiness constantly being promoted remain on the level of secondary needs, the real danger of this moment in history is that people can stay imprisoned in such superficiality and therefore blocked from getting in touch with the primary needs of the human heart. According to the propaganda of consumerism, happiness means "enjoyment as an end in itself", but in fact genuine happiness will come only from "life-styles in which the quest for truth, beauty, goodness and communion with others" are recognised as ways worthy of humanity in its fullness (cf. *Centesimus annus,* 36).

A single struggle: happiness and faith
More and more, as one reflects on this moment of history, it becomes clear that the struggle for happiness and the struggle for faith are two sides of the one coin. Where people are deceived into false or secondary versions of happiness, they are by that fact blocked from reaching anything other than a superficial impression of Christian faith. Where, however, people are liberated from the dominant images and find ways of nourishing the deepest hungers of their hearts, then their roads to happiness will often coincide with roads to faith. The realm of trivial images is a major

source of practical unbelief today. It is a stunting of human poten-
tials. It is a kidnapping of the range of human desire into the
immediate or the transitory. It causes a closing down of hope, a
narrowing of love, a blocking of faith. In this light "practical unbelief" means that the truth revealed in Christ remains simply unreal,
unrecognised and unlived, and this vague situation of non-involve-
ment is now more frequent than the older atheism of an intellectual
or political rejection of God.

> Let others moan about this evil age. I complain of its mean-
> ness, its lack of passion. Life is reduced to one colour.
> Soren Kierkegaard (Nineteenth century
Danish philosopher)

> Mala tempora, laboriosa tempora, hoc dicunt homines. Nos
> sumus tempora, quales sumus, talia sunt tempora.
> [People say, bad times, hard times. We are the age; such as
> we are, such will the age be].
> St Augustine

What has just been described, in brief outline, is a story of a dou-
ble shrinking of a previously broad and rich agenda. If today a
spirit of sheer indifference is the principal enemy of religious faith,
a similar lack of reflection affects the topic of happiness. Where a
culture offers people only trivialised images for their hungers, happiness and faith tend to suffer equally from this confinement of
human vision.

Contrast with the tradition

This chapter has looked at some approaches to happiness that have
been part of relatively recent history – whether during the age of
revolutions or in the revolution in consciousness that is happening
in modern culture. Part of what has been noted in this period has
been a trivialisation of happiness or even its brutalisation under
totalitarian systems. It is interesting also that the topic has not been

at centre stage for thinkers in recent times – as it had been for the ancients and indeed for the great scholastics. To draw this survey of history to a close, it seems helpful to look again at the wealth of that tradition in order to identify some of the impoverishments in thinking that underlie impoverishments in living today.

> Emotivism has become embodied in our culture.
>
> Alisdair MacIntyre (Scottish philosopher)

> The problem is a disintegration in the understanding of the human person. The happiness which is sufficiently rich to correspond to the worth and dignity of the redeemed person is glimpsed only occasionally and vaguely.
>
> Bishop Donal Murray (Ireland)

In the light of the philosophy of human happiness found in Aristotle or Aquinas, it is easier to see through the reductive happiness proposed by the dominant discourse of today's Western culture. The crisis over happiness now is not simply a matter of trivial images, or of a confused culture suffering the pains of so much change. It is not just another variation on the long history of human forgetfulness and distraction from essentials. It involves a basic crisis of meaning and of truth about the human person. Above all it has become culturally difficult, in modern circumstances, to escape from immanentist attitudes, whereby everything, including happiness, is approached subjectively or only from the perspective of human experience here and now. The isolated self becomes *the* measure of values, and here lies a contradiction, because in that loneliness lies a fundamental distortion of perspective.

At the core of the older way of thinking about human happiness lay a sense of purpose and of becoming. This approach explored what goals human beings were meant to pursue. Above all it examined the link between truth and values: it assumed that the ethical task was to identify and follow the true human good. By contrast with this classical model where the self belonged within larger and objective horizons of truth, values, ideals, it is possible to pin-point some of the modern reductions in the agenda of happiness. They include the following deceptive assumptions and tendencies:

1. A belief in fulfilment through the easy spontaneity of experience – an evasion of struggle and of conscience.

2. A belief in a subjective "feels-good" measure of behaviour – a denial of objective values or of the grounding of virtue in truth.

3. A limiting of even generous impulses to the private and domestic spheres – an avoidance of larger purposes and social vision.

4. An assumption that reality coincides with the empirical – and hence a closure towards God and towards mystery.

Deceptive foundations

In the light of this classical tradition of reflecting on happiness and human values, it is easier to discern the comparative impoverishment of the modern agenda on this issue. It has become a trivialised term, more often than not thought of as something random, individualist, and cut off from any sense of the self-transcendent dynamism of the person. The strong bridge between happiness and rational inquiry has collapsed. It has been replaced, so to speak, by a slippery footbridge that can only think of happiness in terms of utility, pleasure, and the private self. As Hamlet might say, "What a falling off is there!"

The next few chapters will show how the "geography" of happiness looks today. Where communism reduced happiness to a materialist goal within an imposed form of society, the phenomenon of consumerism has tended to reduce happiness is a similar way, seeing it in terms of possessions and satisfactions, and leaving to each person the possibility of overcoming this narrowing vision through a personal openness to God.

Reductions of liberalism

> The egoist person, typical of bourgeois society, sees others only in terms of means. Using a now familiar expression, one could say that it involves the order of having rather than of being.
>
> Anton Stres (Slovenian philsopher)

Liberalism develops an immanentist vision of life and its *laissez faire* approach in economics is frequently accompanied by a similar *laissez aller* approach to human values. This policy of non-interference easily slides into a kind of indifference where "anything goes". The net result is frustration of the human desire for roots and meanings, even while providing successfully for surface satisfactions. This reductive tendency reveals itself dramatically in how happiness is often imagined today.

But the narrowing of happiness is not only a matter of economic or political systems, nor is it simply a result of social changes. There is an intellectual root to the crisis concerning happiness. It has to do with how human existence is understood. It has to do with a shrinking in the horizon of human questioning.

It is not wrong, observes *Centesimus annus* (36), echoing *Populorum progressio* (19), to wish to live better; what is wrong is a life-style that is supposed to be better, but in fact is focused towards having rather than being. In this case possessions become the goal of desire and the tendency is to see enjoyment as an end in itself. Similarly, in so far as many modern philosophies have remained closed to metaphysical questions, they have lost contact with a more ancient wisdom concerning happiness.

Unease of modern happiness

Where the thought-patterns of modern culture ignore the spiritual dimension of human beings, this handicap will often be reflected in the more popular embodiments of happiness, as exemplified in everyday behaviour or in the lived assumptions of a society. In short, the spiritual silence of the academy on ultimate issues links

56

up with the religious indifference of the market-place, and all too
often the message of that market-place is that happiness is a matter
of undemanding and transitory experiences. In this way the various influences that form the dominant discourse of modernity all
point in a single direction – towards a shrinking of a great ideal
into smallness and even selfishness. Thus, paradoxically, modern
happiness often remains sated but unsatisfied.

Yet the hope of these pages is positive. If one can understand
better this particular moment in the search for happiness, and if
one can identify some of the forces at work and where they come
from, one will be better able to respond to it wisely. The main danger is that all these pressures can rob people of their roots and
actually cause new unhappiness even while claiming to foster new
forms of freedom and happiness. Their typical thrust is to shift the
language of happiness from such higher values as truth, goodness,
and ultimately faith in God, to immanent goals such as hedonist or
materialist success, or even to more admirable but secondary goals
such as aesthetic enjoyment or interpersonal relationships. But if
these dangers are recognised, and seen as rooted in some of the
lingering ideologies of today's culture, then those dangers become
challenges for dialogue and for liberating response. In this way too
the ground is prepared for an evangelisation of human desire,
which is to be the central theme in the third part of this book.

7

THE GEOGRAPHY OF HAPPINESS: THE POST-COMMUNIST WORLD

Marxism has been a Chernobyl of souls: lies, degrading the person, twisted information, demagogy, manipulation of attitudes, infiltrating other organisations, dark threats of violence. It has stained the heart of Europe with blood.

Josef Zverina (Czech theologian)

People in poor countries look for happiness in terms of social progress, while those in rich countries seek it more in the horizon of the personal. It seems easier to meet the need for bread than the need for love.

Spiro Marasovic (Croatian theologian)

On the day before the publication of his new social encyclical, *Centesimus annus*, Pope John Paul II spoke about it at his weekly general audience and touched on three different contexts in the modern world: the situations where Marxist regimes have recently collapsed, the places where extreme poverty continues to leave entire populations deprived, and the existential confusion so frequent in the wealthiest countries.

Those three worlds suggest a triple structure to the current geography of happiness: it will differ greatly from one setting to another. In a situation of great material poverty, happiness will have a quite different tone from that typical in a situation of universally presumed comfort.

1989 and after

As *Centesimus annus* dramatically highlighted, the year 1989 will surely be remembered as a turning-point in the social, political and religious history for Europe and for the whole world. Many factors converged to make this liberation from oppression possible. But from a religious perspective, the "true cause of the new developments was the spiritual void brought about by atheism". Marxism had promised to eradicate the need for God from the human heart, but the outcome only proves that any success in this way is at the expense of the human heart. Thus this whole enterprise provoked a healthy reaction which often led young people in communist countries to rediscover the person of Christ as meeting "the desire in every human heart for goodness, truth and life" *(CA , 24)*.

This, in brief, is the huge promise opened up by the fall of oppressive regimes, especially in Central Europe. The sheer crudity of the denial of deeper human needs often, paradoxically, helped to keep those needs urgently alive. The absence, even economically, of the more consumerist versions of happiness in a sense protected people from the temptations to superficiality that were so pervasive in the West. Now after 1989 a whole new chapter opens, with many attendant dangers for the trivialisation of happiness and of other human values. But it can also be a moment of new discernment between the rival images of happiness on offer in the expanded market-place of life-styles.

> Journalists were forever asking me if the Christians in the East were better than those in the West. My reply was: "I don't know. I only know that they had less occasions of sin".
>
> Cardinal Joachim Meisner (Archbishop of Cologne)

This moment of challenge for the ex-communist societies provokes various comments and insights from the countries of Central or Eastern Europe. One legacy of marxist dogmatism, as was reported from **Slovenia**, is that people are deeply suspicious about any objective idea of happiness. Authoritarian Marxists provoked so much scepticism in the past that now people are easy prey to a vague liberalism.

In **Bohemia** communism has caused a massive pollution of human values, a damage to the trust people have in institutions, and in general an acceptance of dishonest and corrupt ways of acting in society. Thus communism has ruined not only the economy but has left a stigma on people's sense of morality and leaves them deeply suspicious of any political leaders.

Illusions of quick success
The advent of new freedom, in **Hungary** for instance, awakens some attractive illusions about an easy happiness being available. Far from freedom being synonymous with happiness, this new openness can prove to be a time of confusion, when people seek happiness in irresponsible ways previously closed to them. In the course of frenzied shopping trips to Austria, Hungarians spent millions of dollars in a short time, most of it on luxury items such as video recorders or microwave ovens.

In the **Soviet Union** in particular, the sudden lifting of controls has led to many sad excesses – in violence, crime, alcoholism, drug addiction, even murder. It seems reminiscent, as one person put it, of the boiling over of a saucepan when the lid comes off. This ferment finds parallels even in the world of spiritual searching for happiness, where the menu is wide and somewhat confused.

From **Poland** came reports of both negative and positive perceptions of the Church over the question of happiness. On the one hand, some young people have a poor experience of religious practices and think of religion as pessimistic and restrictive. On the other hand, within recent history it is a source of strength and hope for the future that the Church has been so visible in the defence of human rights. In this way people see how the gospel fully lived, as well as being a grace of transformation for individuals, is a powerful source of happiness even in the social field.

In general the collapse of Marxism has not led automatically to a recovery of religious faith or to an easy victory over practical materialism. Without the religious dimension, it was claimed from **East Germany**, a person will inevitably fulfil his or her hungers in some horizontal direction. Unfortunately nowadays in the ex-communist areas the opium of the people can be literally opium, or one of its obvious substitutes, including the occult. Or else they fall into the idolatry of worshipping the West as a kind of paradise.

Perhaps one of the saddest legacies of communism has been a cynicism or indifference towards human values, and certainly this seems to be one outcome when people suffer distortion of their hunger for happiness: empty shops and emptied spirits.

> People under totalitarian dictatorships developed a flourishing culture of love, the solidarity of the persecuted. In the new free market economy will this solidarity give way to a fight of each one for oneself? All of a sudden Liberalism has become the most popular ideology in these countries.
>
> László Lukács (Hungarian philosopher)

> Breaking out of the house of slavery does not mean an immediate entrance into the Promised Land, but rather a painful pilgrimage through the desert.
>
> Tomás Halík (Czech theologian)

After the euphoria of liberation the previously communist countries have run into many tough challenges and painful transitions. The collapse of the older ideologies of state socialism has left people morally endangered in new and perhaps unexpected ways. Where will their happiness be found now? In so far as the new external freedoms can go hand in hand with a spiritual void, the gift of freedom can shrink into mere drifting, individualist and egoist. *The* danger is that a crude ideology of Marxism may be replaced with a more attractive but equally dehumanising ideology of Liberalism. Where this occurs, it brings about a tragic stunting of the agenda of human happiness: people are quietly robbed of the full range of their humanity with its deeper needs for love, social vision and, ultimately, transcendent faith.

Dangers and challenges

But clearly the positive challenge is stronger than the shadows in these ex-communist societies. In the words of Pope John Paul II, "for some countries of Europe the real post-war period is just beginning", and in this delicate moment of history "a great effort is needed to rebuild morally and economically" (*Centesimus annus*, 27-28). A struggle between two embodiments of happiness will be part of that process of reconstruction. On the one hand there is the lure of surface fashions and of money-based satisfactions, and they are all the more attractive because under the old regimes they have been denied for so long. On the other hand people can have the courage to choose a different path towards forms of happiness that meet the depth of the human heart.

It is a crossroads moment for what was previously the so-called Second World. As the Russian writer Vladimir Zelinski has remarked, the image of the West is now a powerful presence on the stage of his country's history: no amount of warnings or denunciations will stop people looking to the West as a "promised land".

The joyous chant of Alleluia

Great therefore is the challenge for the West. The European Synod of Bishops declared this in no uncertain manner: the collapse of the communist system, which was so rapid and truly extraordinary, was due in large measure to the heroic witness of the Christian churches. Even for many non-believers it was viewed almost in terms of a "miracle", and for many Christians as a genuine "Kairos" in the history of salvation, and as a great challenge to continue the innovative work of God.

"In the night", wrote the Slovenian poet Edvard Kocbek in his diary for Holy Week, 12 April 1952, "I hear by radio the joyous and solemn chant of Alleluia. At once a huge joy sweeps over me, the joy of living Catholicism, of a great Church, saving, alive, in spite of its earthly weight and its decadence. God, with all my being, I thank you on my knees for the grace that you grant me, nourishing me with your salvation".

8

SITUATIONS IN THE DEVELOPING WORLD

In many regions of Africa one finds remarkable signs of vitality, of joy for life, which contrast with a certain pessimism, a widespread egoism, and even a spiritual tiredness in the more economically developed societies.

Cardinal Josef Tomko (Czechoslovakia)

The African philosophy of happiness is expressed in the adage: "I am because we are". . .We belong together in kinship.

Joseph Kariuki (Kenyan theologian)

The Christian response to the search for happiness has not yet found its language for the emerging culture of the city, with all its possibilities of alienation and disillusioned loneliness.

Bishop Antonio do Carmo Cheuiche (Brazil)

Even Aristotle remarked that in situations of deprivation, people will naturally and even rightly identify happiness with meeting their urgent material needs. But in all the reports from the Third World today, there is complementary and more positive light on happiness. Again and again there were descriptions of how poorer people manage to preserve a sense of community that is often lost in the richer parts of the planet. Perhaps here the literal meaning of the word companionship becomes relevant, for more deprived settings often witness the generosity of sharing the little bread available. To say this should in no way diminish the horror and the shock at the fact that "perhaps the majority today" remain in a "state of humiliating subjection" (*Centesimus annus*, 33). But it does bring out another and complementary message concerning happiness.

Four constant themes

A brief geography of happiness as found in various developing countries highlights the huge diversity of situations that the Church is faced with, and also points to a certain convergence of experiences. There are various areas of crisis or disturbance:

1. The often rapid and disordered move from rural to urban living has left people uprooted and poorer in community supports.
2. Even greater gaps are opening between rich and poor, both internationally and within the Third World countries between majority poor and minority privileged.
3. Traditional religious belonging is often disturbed by an invasion of new sects.
4. An explosion of alien images through television is having a secularising and cheapening impact on people's values and hopes.

A frighteningly high proportion of young people in **Uruguay** are estimated to use drugs at some stage between the ages of fourteen and twenty-nine and this seems in tune with the general tendency to replace relationships and commitments with consumerist "well-being" and the right to pleasure on all levels. Another powerful element in Uruguayan youth culture is the phenomenon of collective events connected with popular music.

Happiness through family love, friendship, solidarity

In spite of all the tensions within **Chile**, as well as sources of disturbance from abroad, ranging from the troublesome influence of "evangelical" proselytism to the secularising impact of influences from the rich world, it is still true that the vast majority of people continue to seek the meaning of life through religion.

In **Mexico** it is among the simplest and poorest people that the happiness of faith in Christ is often most transparently glimpsed. But among the new populations of the vast cities religion is not even seen as an obstacle to happiness: it simply does not count in the lives of many.

In **Indonesia** happiness is thought of mainly in communal

terms, and not as a matter of individual or personal fulfilment. The old roots of solidarity through family, tribal, village or neighbourhood communities are still central in how people seek to build happy lives.

Apart from the typical problems of false happiness associated with excesses of egoism – drugs, alcohol, power, consumerism – in **Angola** some are finding new happiness through living out the social teaching of the Church in the service of the deprived – in ministries of health or education, or in working with refugees or orphans.

A Muslim poet from **Bangladesh** has claimed that it is the natural thing for people to find happiness through coming together in communion and friendship. What is lacking is simply the creating of possibilities for this to happen. Authentic human contact is the door to preserving genuine happiness and to saving people from false forms of satisfaction.

In Africa *the* key to happiness lies in family life and in the presence of children. In **Kenya,** for instance, fecundity is viewed as essential to happiness and a couple's inability to have children is seen as a major tragedy. The Western emphasis on individual fulfilment is something alien to the African mentality with its inclination towards communal events and celebrations. Even death is approached as a family occasion for reconciliation.

> In Korea it is a source of unending wonder to see how joyfully our people respond to the simplest pleasures. In a society with profound rural roots of recent memory, the fundamental happiness of a good harvest remains alive as an image of happiness, although for many, children are now the only remaining form of harvest.
>
> Cardinal Stephen Kim (Archbishop of Seoul)

Korea echoes some of the characteristics of Africa or Latin America. In spite of what Cardinal Kim describes as an appalling burden of poverty for many, the values of friendship and family life continue to be central for most people. Even excesses in drink or in the pursuit of money are not unconnected with celebrating life or in seeking to provide security for the family. In such a context, it is worth recalling, the quest for happiness is influenced by memories of intense suffering and deprivation.

In the culture of **Madagascar** materialism of an un-Western kind can be found. In traditional religion and anthropology there would be much less of a firm distinction between "having" and "being" than is usual in European thinking. The ideal of wealth is deeply ingrained in people's approach to happiness, and is embodied in many sayings and in traditional poetry. "In a potato field, the spade follows the tubers and the people follow the one who has money". Such an ambiguous desire for possessions is a crucial element in the assumptions of this society, and is rendered more problematic by both poverty and the arrival of modern consumerism.

> Tranquillity at home and peace with God were part of the rural Filipino's idea of happiness . . .The rich urban Filipino tends to be like Americans or Europeans. Happiness for him tends to be identified with wealth so as to be able to enjoy the products of a consumer society.
>
> Paul Dumol (Filipino playwright)

> Our peasants have a deep desire for a fullness of happiness rooted in trust in God as Father. Colombians of the upper class reflect many of the features of modern culture: narcissistic individualism, success at any price, and hardly any social sensibility.
>
> Bishop Darío Castrillón Hoyos (Colombia)

A very similar contrast of attitude is described in both of these quotations, even though they come from different continents – from the **Philippines** and from **Colombia** respectively. Both offer evidence of how society in developing countries is becoming increasingly split between rich and poor and, in a parallel fashion, pluralist as regards moral values.

Colombia exemplifies a diversity of social groupings: the new city dwellers who are in danger of losing their religious roots under the pressures of immediacy, the workers who simply give all their energies to money-making, and the student generation who lose touch with the happiness of the gospels under the influence of a certain scepticism and suspicion induced by some modern philosophies. But not all is negative. Many young people are also discovering the joy of a generous option for the poor and one which often includes a strong sense of sharing the Cross of Christ.

Equador reveals a similar diversity as regards happiness with four distinct groupings: *wealthy minorities* were marked by a closed individualism and a fetish of power and of accumulating money; *peasants and the urban poor* find happiness in less individualistic forms, positively through mutual solidarity and celebration, but negatively through escapism in alcohol, prostitution, and even in some "religious" practices tinged with superstition; *communities of committed Christians* where happiness is explicitly linked to engaging in the struggle of Christ's Kingdom in this world, especially through some preferential option for the poor; *fundamentalist Christian sects* who seek happiness through strong group identity and a certain religious commitment.

In all these countries the culture of mutual giving and of communion, found in the sacrifices and in daily commitments for the common good, shows forth a living witness of the Church and a Christian source of happiness in all environments.

9

HAPPINESS IN THE FIRST WORLD

We hold these truths to be sacred and undeniable: that all men are created equal and independent, that from that equal creation they derive rights inherent and inalienable, among which are the preservation of life, and liberty, and the pursuit of happiness.

Thomas Jefferson (Nineteenth century US President)

In both Eastern and Western Europe "power" has destroyed layers of depth in the human person . . . But in practice the methods in the West have been much more successful in obliterating human conscience.

Bishop Francisco Javier Martínez (Spain)

In the varied language of happiness now, immanental and hedonistic tendencies seem especially strong in the wealthier countries of the world. There is a sense in which today's most powerful interpretations of happiness – literally beamed through television from the richer world into the homes of countless people in less privileged situations – are controlled by the "image industry" of that rich world. If trivialisation reigns in the First World, this contagion is likely to spread to the rest of the planet. Such is the "global village" in which values are so rapidly shaped and communicated now.

But it would be quite wrong to judge this complex world of change in an exclusively negative way. What is required is a balanced discernment of the influences at work.

When a society becomes economically prosperous and living standards reach levels where almost all material needs are satisfied. . . people begin to seek different happiness-values which tend to be more "psychological" or "spiritual", moving from "steadiness-orientation to "leisure-orientation".

Iwao Munakata (Japanese sociologist)

Several inquiries have highlighted a change in the hierarchy of values: in the wealthier sections of the population, diligence, efficiency, order and correctness have given way to a hedonistic and post-materialistic tendency, which gives more value to leisure, pleasure and participation in decisions.

Bernhard Grom (German philosopher)

Japan and Germany

It is significant that such similar points of view are reported from two of the leading industrial countries of the world, **Japan** and **Germany** respectively. Both situations report a disenchantment with crude money-making or with a merely material level of success. These are seen as not constituting a genuine happiness. From Japan the clear message was of a turning towards post-material values since about 1985, and of a clearer realisation of the cultural price that has been paid for economic success in terms of a painful "social disintegration". People discovered that they were "losing fundamental cultural symbols and values" without finding real substitutes. Recent times have witnessed the erosion of a rootedness previously found through extended family structures and also of village-style loyalties which had managed to survive even the transfer to an industrial setting. The new model of happiness for the Japanese seems to be at once more individualistic and more spiritually searching. One university student claimed that seeking out a personal meaning for life would involve waking "from the dream based on science and technology and rediscovering the essential nature of humanity".

As it happens, the questionnaire of the Pontifical Council was published in a Japanese cultural journal, *Shung-ju,* and elicited 102 responses, many from non-Christian students. Here again the evidence pointed to a significant shift in the ways in which happiness is being sought. At least for some of these students it was primarily of the "heart", and therefore their goals were changing from the visible and material to the invisible. Side by side with a world that offered many materialistic and hedonistic satisfactions, some of these young people stressed rather their need for love and friendship as core values. Faced with so many pressures, many of them expressed a deep confusion: "We have such a flood of material things that nobody quite knows what he likes or what he needs or what he wants to do".

The German situation, in a remarkably similar way, shows many young adults in search of new values and of an alternative life style beyond mere materialism. If one were to imagine, so to speak, a compass of happiness for today, then in the most economically successful countries the needle is pointing more towards personal values than towards possessions. A sense of satisfaction with one's own life, often connected with marriage or family, seems to be coming back to the centre of attention. Feelings are acknowledged as central to individual development. People today are much more "romantic" than in previous ages in that an ideal of love has come to be central for happiness today, in a way that was unknown hitherto. However, the love in question is nearly always thought of in terms of man-woman relationships, and seldom in terms of parents, children, or community.

In this connection one must also mention the explosion of interest in recent decades in such areas as self-fulfilment therapies, "self-help" versions of secularised spirituality, and developments that link up with "New Age" trends of thought, which will be given more attention in Part Three of this book.

Ireland and Australia

The structures of modern, technological society tend towards a kind of anonymity, a kind of suppression of the individual. This can be seen in the area of work and unemployment. The lack of a coherent vision of the person is what allows modern society to see itself as little more than an economic system.

Bishop Donal Murray (Ireland)

The typical churchless Australian heart is a compound of natural good-will and unreconstructed original sin. A society largely given over to self-concern is particularly liable to be invaded by a sense of meaninglessness.

Archbishop Eric D'Arcy (Australia)

These statements come from a small country and a vast country at opposite ends of the globe – **Ireland** and **Australia**. According to various surveys available, both nations would rate themselves as successful in offering people happiness, and yet they both report shadows of a new kind. From Ireland came descriptions of a sense of powerlessness affecting people: they often feel helpless before the forces which shape their lives, and even in this country of exceptionally high religious practice, ever larger tracts of life are lived in an atmosphere of practical atheism. Crucial areas such as education and health, although the Church continues to have a high profile here, seem in danger of being taken over by a technological and soulless mentality. Although people can see that material success does not provide a deep happiness, they can lack the will or the courage to fight the dehumanising forces around. Thus happiness retreats into the private realm.

Australians, partly by reason of a climate that differs somewhat from that of Ireland, give special emphasis to outdoor and leisure activities as vehicles of happiness. But in many recent surveys the top domain has been satisfaction with family life, especially children, followed by friendships, and only after these did people mention money, sex, health and other more external measurements of success. Once again it seems in line with a certain post-materialist revaluing of issues, as was reported from Japan and Germany.

In this respect, Archbishop D'Arcy cited a moment from the film *Sex, Lies and Videotape* where a woman patient is questioned by a psychotherapist about happiness. She seems bewildered and interrupts him: "What's so marvellous about happiness? Last time I was happy I put on five pounds", and the remark seemed to capture a new cynicism that is also present in highly developed societies. In this light the average Australian was described as quite "secular" but not "anti-religious". Out of this situation that unites secularised consciousness with relatively privileged standards of living new forms of the quest for happiness emerge, such as tourism as a possible quest for the strange and even the transcendent. But the danger here, as in many pleasant distractions, is of stopping short at a level of mere self-concern. As an Australian non-believer remarked, critiques of hedonism and materialism recognise that one cannot obtain happiness by aiming directly at it. Instead, out of all the disappointments with easily available surface happiness in rich societies, perhaps an old truth is being rediscovered in new ways: that happiness can only emerge as a by-product of dedication to other people or of commitment to something larger than self-concern.

Italy

> Images of happiness are always culturally conditioned.
> Cardinal Silvano Piovanelli (Archbishop of Florence)

> People of today are convinced that happiness here and now is an absolute right and that therefore no sacrifices of any kind should be involved.
> Gian Paolo Salvini (Editor of *Civiltà Cattolica*)

From much of the more "developed" world come comments about the shrinking of the agenda of happiness under the influence of modern publicity for the consumerist life-style – a phenomenon that has been a concern of the Church for some time now. In 1975 Pope Paul VI discerned a new face to atheist secularism in the existence of a "consumer society" with "the pursuit of pleasure set up as the supreme value" (*Evangelii nuntiandi,* 55). More than a decade later, Pope John Paul II pointed to the stark contrast in our world between the "underdevelopment" of so many poor countries and the "overdevelopment" of others characterised by "excessive availability of all kinds of material goods". Twice in that same passage the Holy Father added that this accumulation of consumerist opportunities can never open the door to "genuine happiness" *(Sollicitudo rei socialis,* 1987, 28).

Within recent decades **Italy** has known a certain sense of pride at having emerged from centuries where the mass of people lived in poverty. In theory many Italians would insist that money is not the key to happiness but in practice most people act as if material well-being is at least the essential basis for a happy life. When asked for their views on happiness, perhaps a majority would give more emphasis to freedom as an essential factor, but in practice this usually seems to be interpreted in terms of a rather individualistic freedom. Italy would echo the tendency, already noted in other developed countries, for the focus of happiness to shift from material to "immaterial" goods, such as culture, music, videos, sport, and a wide range of other leisure pursuits. Connected with this trend is a decrease in the value placed on work. Indeed Italy has a high level of absenteeism from work, and often without any genuine excuse being offered.

From the younger generations of Italians there is a confused rather than a uniform message. On the one hand there seems to be a certain pessimism, especially about having children. Italy now has the lowest birth rate within the European Community – and this in a country that had the reputation of a particular love for children and family. The contrast with Africa is quite striking here. This lessening in traditional values is accompanied by a frenetic escapism: relative to the young population, Italy has one of the highest proportions of discotheques in the world, together with an alarming number of deaths from road accidents as young people return from these discos in the early hours of the morning. On the other hand, Italy has probably the world's highest proportion of young people involved in voluntary work of various kinds, as well as an impressive number of Church-based lay movements.

Even the admirable dedication shown in the voluntary service of others can mask a certain unsureness about permanent commitment of any kind, and, if so, this reticence seems typical of modern culture. Clearly, such shyness over a lasting involvement affects both marriage and religious vocations today. More generally, many people seem to stand at the threshold of commitment but are hesitant about a more sure and permanent "yes" to God. In short, the avenue to human happiness represented by the giving of a whole life is shadowed by new doubts in modern circumstances and this is particularly true of the more developed world.

Spain

> The postmodern attitude is suspicious of such traditional values as work, personal effort, or all motivating systems seeking a better world. It is a void of values.
>
> Antonio Vásquez (Spanish philosopher)

> Most people in our cultural context do not feel happy, but neither do they feel wretched: they inhabit an ambiguous twilight zone that lacks desire or hope.
>
> Jaime García (Spanish theologian)

The **Spanish** situation is marked by the dramatic cultural changes experienced there within the last decade or so, changes that have brought about a major change in the "tone" of happiness. This period has witnessed an explosion of doubt concerning traditional institutions of all kinds – family, school, state, church. It has also been a time of collapse of many moral values. Underlying all this commentators have diagnosed a significant break in ways of thinking and feeling. There has been a rupture between public and private life, and likewise between "instrumental" activities such as work and all forms of organisation, and "expressive" activities marked by creativity, spontaneity and various quests for personal liberation.

This major shift has also been described as the difference between modernity and post-modernity, that is, between a culture where a liberal tradition of rationality held sway and where efficiency and planning were valued, and a rather different culture that has little time for the great questions of life, that finds rationality stifling, and which retreats to a fragmented life of sophisticated self-fulfilment in many forms. Behind this post-modern life-style lies uncertainty about the very worthwhileness of existence – which is a different version of unhappiness than was previously encountered in Spain.

Great Britain, Austria, New Zealand

One may contrast this analysis with the situation in **Great Britain,** a country with a much longer history of secularisation and of modernisation. There the search for happiness is often expressed in quite materialistic terms, but on reflection it seems that this façade may not represent the full quest that is going on. Underneath the seemingly superficial satisfactions, perhaps people have deeper and even some more generous goals: a quest for self-fulfilment, a varied life, the freedom to live freely according to one's own values, becoming happy through good, fulfilling relationships and becoming a better person.

In countries as far apart as **Austria** and **New Zealand** a new focus on physical health is found as part of the contemporary search for happiness. In both cases it was connected with a search for alternative or counter-cultural life-styles, and a new spirit of therapeutic naturalism. The phenomenon of "jogging" seems ambiguous in some respects. It can be admirable in terms of self-control and as expressing "holistic" reverence for the body. It can embody a genuine critique of indulgent and opulent ways of life. But it can also symbolise an egocentric culture, where isolated self-fulfilment becomes an obsession and something closed to both spiritual and social consciousness.

France

> People speak a lot about the quality of life but in fact this quality tends to show itself more through having than through being. Perhaps the emphasis on ecology represents a certain openness to being.
>
> Archbishop Jacques Jullien (France)

> This quest for quality of life has an aspect of wisdom that cannot be denied, especially in its renewed attention to personal relationships.
>
> Jacques Sommet (French Jesuit writer)

In **France** there has been considerable debate, at least over the last decade, about the death of ideology and the birth of a new narcissistic self. Many people no longer trust the big visions or any claims about large-scale collective change. Instead they have retreated to the privatised world of their own self, becoming concerned with their health, their bodies, their homes, and so they remain preoccupied with small things within a self-enclosed universe. Happiness therefore becomes a matter of satisfactions within a narrow compass. Sincerity replaces truth. Immediacy is preferred to commitment. Rights take over from duties or sacrifices. Leisure ousts political action. Society exists to help "me". Being at home with oneself, with a certain harmony "within one's own skin", becomes the measure of happiness. Various studies of this situation have pointed to the erosion of social identity and the disenchanted and private horizons that characterise a new narcissism.

Other voices have sought to qualify this picture, or at least to offer alternative and more positive interpretations. Thus the results of a 1988 survey on happiness revealed that 89% of French people would describe themselves as happy and that this rises to a striking 96% for young people. Allowing for the limitations of such surveys, the percentages remain impressive. Moreover, the largest single reason given is hardly classifiable as narcissistic: 59% identified a warm family environment as the basis of their happiness.

Concern with quality of life seems to have replaced a merely materialistic or economic yardstick of happiness. Perhaps the word "satisfaction" indicates better the tone of the culture than the word "happiness". People seem to be searching for a certain new fullness, a way of managing their lives so as to balance their various needs – physical, intellectual, affective. The previous dominance by the world of technology and of work seems to be on the wane, as people put more emphasis on personal space of various kinds.

Canada, United States, Holland

> Our culture is one of images, not ideas. What people want in a witness is a human being in the process of becoming human . . . They want witnesses who are respectful of the created universe and for whom environmental concern is not a fad.
>
> Archbishop Marcel Gervais (Canada)

> In the development of human understanding, new forms of therapy make possible a compassionate and sometimes healing approach to problems that were considered intractable several generations ago.
>
> Lawrence C. Brennan (American Vincentian theologian)

> "Material private happiness" is not the all-encompassing goal of humans. A lively social consciousness is also present, in which the happiness of the other and the welfare of all are prominent. It would be unjust to assume that people are only out for their own material advantage.
>
> Bert Schumacher (Dutch sociologist)

These three quotations, two from **North America** and the third from **Holland**, add to what has just been summarised from France, and they capture a certain optimism concerning happiness. They freely admit that much of the so-called "progress" of the wealthy world can be in a silly and even irresponsible direction, or that many people in the richer nations seem to live for comforts of a selfish and private kind.

The positive and relatively new features of happiness found in the First World can be summarised under four headings: a spirit of *generosity,* now linked with a sense of responsibility for the whole world community; a new conscience about *care for creation* and for the planet earth; a trust in *pragmatism* and in the scientific tradition, applying this in a spirit of hope to many human issues; a commitment to *human dignity.*

These qualities indicate a new groping towards positive values. Even if the cult of self-development is not without ambiguity, it is important that many people today put a great emphasis on the process of slowly and patiently becoming human. In more religious language, all those four positive attitudes speak of conversion: a conversion from mere egoism to wanting to build a more just world; a conversion from carelessness about the earth to a new and responsible ecology; a conversion from utilitarian and mechanical approaches to a desire to make technology serve real human needs; and a conversion from fatalism or passivity to a sense of gratitude for each person and a desire to live the gift of existence to the full.

In spite of the many impoverishments and superficialities that can masquerade as happiness, there are signs of the times that give food for hope as well, and on that note it is ripe to turn to the specifically religious and Christian dimensions of happiness.

Part Three

EVANGELISATION OF DESIRE

10

WHAT ARE YOU LOOKING FOR?

We are all well aware of the illusions which Eros dangles
before our eyes: we know how far its illusory "eternity" is
from a definitive decision in self-renouncing love.

Hans Urs von Balthasar (Swiss theologian)

The Good News must bring about change. Communication
tells the story, and it is the story that changes people. This
communication and change is wrought not merely by the
words used, but also by the joy of our lives.

Paul Williamson (Marist priest, New Zealand)

The title of this chapter comes from an early moment in the gospel
of John. In fact it tells of the first meeting recorded between Jesus
and any of his disciples, and the words are his first spoken words
in this gospel of many conversations. The situation is simple: John
the Baptist had his own circle of disciples and on this particular
day he points Jesus out to two of them. He has already told them
that the whole purpose of his life is to prepare people for a greater
One who is to come. Now that person has come. So the two disciples, Andrew and John, leave John the Baptist and begin to follow
Jesus – literally walking behind him.

It is at this point that Jesus turns around and puts this basic
question to the two disciples about what is the central hope of their
hearts. It is not a question that can be asked out of the blue of a
stranger in the street. Indeed, in this short episode of the gospel, it
is a moment that has been long prepared through their companionship with John the Baptist, so that now at last they are ripe to begin
to get in touch with their deepest longings. "What are you looking
for?" is one the most fundamental and most personal questions
about life.

> Joy and an extraordinary expansion of the person are found at the heart of the "Good News" of the Gospel. But against the tide of our merely human longings and desires, enclosed within a purely worldly horizon. Not necessarily a radical contradiction. But certainly a radical conversion.
>
> René Coste (French theologian)

John the Baptist has prepared his disciples to be open to this question in a new way. The coming of Jesus invites those two disciples to recognise their hungers for happiness in a new light, ultimately in his light. And when they "come" and "see" and "stay" with him, they are entering a new way of discipleship, whereby their desires are liberated and fulfilled by his happiness. The words which Jesus will speak at the Last Supper could be applied to this much earlier moment of encounter: "Let my joy be in you and your joy will be full". This initial meeting is also a meeting between two joys, between their desire and his gift, between their hunger and the fulfilment that is offered through faith in him.

In the light of this scene one can see Christian happiness being discovered in three stages: preparation of desire, recognition of desire, evangelisation of desire.

Three pastoral stages

The first task is to get in touch with the depth of the human longing for happiness, and to do so beyond its frequent trivialisation under the pressures of modern culture. This is comparable to the ministry of John the Baptist with those two disciples: he had prepared them to be able to hear that question of Jesus, "What do you want?" and to hear it at a level worthy of their humanity.

The second task is to recognise what that question raises – the main desire of the heart. The issue of happiness – as has been seen so often in these pages – touches and is connected with all the major issues of meaning and values in our time.

The third necessity is to free this desire from reductive prisons and to evangelise it for a fullness of life and love. This is a central spiritual adventure for each person and for each culture.

The atheistic ideologies of the 19th and 20th centuries have resulted in a deep distrust towards any religious position.

Bishop René Rakotondrabe (Madagascar)

For non-believers, religious hopes are not felt to be necessary for happiness – not even for maintaining one's happiness in the face of the inevitable and final dissolution of death.

Michael Mason (Australian writer)

Turning to today's situation, it would seem that with all the changes of the last few decades there has arisen a serious split between religion and life, which is more acute in some parts of the world than in others. Or, perhaps more accurately, there is a gap between how religion is *perceived* by many people and how they *perceive* the needs of their lives. The dialogue to which the Church is called involves a careful listening to such anxieties and disappointments. It asks also for a renewal of gospel joy.

In fact two important difficulties arise when one asks about happiness in relation to the Christian vision today. The first involves a rift between the language of faith and the dominant language of modern culture. The second is a danger from an opposite direction. It involves a new tendency where people fulfil their spiritual needs by merging religion and life in a very subjective way. They approach religion as something individually useful, or as a source of psychological security, with the result that in practice they forget the transcendence of God and the reality of Revelation.

On the one hand religion can be viewed as something utterly irrelevant to happiness. On the other hand a certain religiousness can be cultivated as an important component in human happiness. But both tendencies, though different in approach, risk being ruled by a similar spirit of secularism. Whenever the transcendent vision of faith weakens, and whenever a mainly anthropological mentality takes over, either religion will fade into the distance as something unreal, or else the language of religion will be adapted to meet genuine personal needs but in a merely humanist way. In both instances the hunger for happiness is secularised. In one situation it loses contact with religion and even sees it as an enemy to happiness. In the other situation the quest for happiness expresses itself in pseudo-religious forms, whose latent denial of God can be hard to discern.

> While the Church is the true mediator of happiness, the way in which she preaches the "Word" is often seen to be remote from the human heart. People experience the Church's presentation of the Good News as obscuring the very vision of happiness it is striving to communicate.
>
> Joseph Dargan (Major Religious Superiors, Ireland)

> The whole of humanity today is a huge orphanage where millions of people are deemed to be without creator, without redeemer, without father. Do they suffer because of this? Some do. But mostly they are like birds whose wings were gnawed away at birth. They were made to fly but they don't know it.
>
> Patrick du Ruffray (French writer)

Levels of religious maturity

Whether or not religion seems to nourish happiness will depend to a large degree on the quality of a person's religious belonging. If someone has the benefit of a personal level of religious formation, this will surely help to promote a sense of happiness. On the other hand, if a person lacks opportunities for spiritual development and remains dependent on a merely inherited set of beliefs and practices, this situation is less likely to lead to happiness through religion. Perhaps especially in today's culture, many of the traditional modes of external religious belonging have diminished in fruitfulness – because they are now in competition with a much more complex environment of culture. The village mentality is lost, in every sense, in the urbanised context. Hence religious practices that remain ritualistic or impersonal or passive will seldom be sources of happiness in today's sophisticated world. A gap opens up between the world of religion and the world of reality, and unless it is bridged the notion of "happiness" will seem to have little to do with "religion".

As might be expected from the earlier survey of the "geography" of happiness, such a distance between faith and life can take several forms: in Third World situations it is often the rich who are more formalistic but practising in a minimum way, whereas the poor may suffer rather from a religion of fear, tinged with a certain superstition. By contrast, in some communist-dominated countries – or now ex-communist as the case may be – religion has been the target for hostile propaganda from many sources. It was constantly portrayed as an enemy to happiness, or as offering only the illusion of a happiness beyond the grave. Marxist theory always recognised the basic quest for happiness in humanity but usually saw religion as a key example of alienated happiness. Perhaps another dimension of marxist propaganda has had a more subtle and damaging effect – the stress on this world as the only possible horizon of happiness. If God has been banished and if we human beings are seen as the only source of salvation within history, once the political system changes this approach can easily swing over into a merely consumerist pursuit of happiness – as already seen.

> Atheism in the United States arises from a climate of mind which makes the authority of experience depend upon those methods that took their rise from the physical and biological sciences.
>
> Michael J. Buckley (American theologian)

> The West has finally achieved human rights, and even to excess, but the human sense of responsibility to God and society has grown dimmer and dimmer.
>
> Alexander Solzhenitsyn (Russian novelist)

Religion marginalised

From *India*, clearly a different cultural setting for religion, it is reported that another version of this gap exists. In so far as the sacred is presented as a very separate world, it remains cut off from the pressures of reality. Religion appears too legalistic, too rigid and too other-worldly to have much to do with happiness. As modernisation increases, religions are increasingly felt to fail human needs, and to lose credibility because they remain on the level of rituals for special occasions. Something of the same pattern recurs, in a different way, in some more "advanced" societies today, where religion is often perceived as a source of restriction rather than of happiness. The freedom in question may be open to critique, but the net result is that religion loses its fundamental meaning – *re-ligio* – of connectedness and is regarded by some people with growing mistrust.

> Modern times have often experienced a sense of a conflictual relationship between God and humanity.
> Cardinal Jean-Marie Lustiger (Archbishop of Paris)

> Between the sage and the saint there is no opposition.
> Jean Festugière (French Dominican scholar)

One version of the separation between religion and human happiness is rooted in the vague atmosphere of religious indifference present in many modernised societies. Often this phenomenon is also the product of an impoverished encounter with religion. Where people have never experienced religion or church except in formal and institutionalised ways, it is understandable that they sense a distance between what they perceive in religion and their so-called real lives.

A second type of divorce between religion and happiness stems from overt philosophies of a militant kind. Even if atheistic attacks on religion have become out-dated and infrequent, a more subtle hostility to religion can be found in the images of the mass media. A tone of cynicism pervades and religion is often portrayed as either morally negative or just humanly boring.

Rediscovery of link with happiness

But positive news emerges also from today's complex world. Much depends, for instance, on the *quality* of a person's encounter with faith. If people experience a living community of believers, a committed parish, a way of growth in prayer, some attractive expression of the intellectual tradition of Christianity, the witness of believers serving the weak and deprived . . . or any of the many living anchors of faith ancient and ever new, then they will find religion and happiness to be profoundly connected for them.

In this respect, it is interesting to note that a 1990 survey in France revealed that 72% of "believers" saw God as "Good News for all" and that 58% would claim that God made them happy. According to these figures the majority of believers seem to have a largely positive experience of faith, and it is clear that this is true elsewhere as well.

Within the different setting of North America, it seems that the newer generations feel less of a dichotomy between happiness here and hereafter than was previously the case. The dominant understanding now is of complementarity between two modes of happiness. Nor do people view the Church as interested only in the after-life. In general the Gospel is seen as genuinely good news and Christian faith as making a positive and even essential contribution to human fulfilment in this life. But one qualification should be added: because there is so much television evangelism and so many examples of superficial religion, many North Americans are also wary of the deceptions and self-righteousness of some "conversions", and of their claims to being *the* way to happiness. Within North American culture the person of Christ is almost universally reverenced, but suspicion lingers about the ambiguity of religion, which can be either authentic and beneficial or destructive and downright dangerous. Since experience is the new measure for authenticity, it is precisely in this dimension that religion leaves many people dissatisfied. They are looking for something that reaches them more deeply. In particular, they are impressed by something visibly lived rather than by anything spoken of in words alone. It is indeed a source of contagious happiness when people today come into contact with faith truly alive in action.

> There is a broad and widespread desire to relate to God in a very positive way which takes a variety of forms. There is also the growing realization that moral values contribute to human happiness.
>
> Roland J. Faley (Conference of Major Superiors, USA)

> I am convinced that proclaiming the Good News as a source of happiness has hardly any chance of being heard by modern man, unless it starts from questioning the presuppositions of a purely human happiness rooted in a closed form of immanence.
>
> Henrique de Lima Vaz (Brazilian Jesuit philosopher)

It is becoming clear that a major source of a split between religion and happiness comes from a poor level of evangelisation and hence a level of faith development that leaves people immature for today's situation. Many people have never had much opportunity, or at least not taken the opportunity, to grasp the riches of Christian faith and of its vision of happiness. So the main operative influence on their lives will be the powerful secular images and assumptions that surround them. It is small wonder if this combination of religious ignorance and of secularist pressures leaves them incapable of seeing the happiness offered by Christian faith.

In this respect, a particularly sensitive difficulty concerns the question of sexuality. It is an area where values have declined, especially in the more developed countries, and one where deep issues are at stake. Therefore it is vitally important that the Church's position and teaching should appear in its fullness. Frequently the Church is wrongly viewed as rigid, out-of-touch, and judgemental in areas of morality related to marriage. Where a certain liberal mentality dominates, religion is often portrayed as being at odds with human happiness, and this would affect not only agnostics or the non-practising baptised, but many who want to remain active Church members.

It could be a surprise for them to learn the extent to which the Church has a rich theology of the body and of human love. Because of so much reductiveness concerning sexuality in the contemporary world, it becomes vital for the Church to be known as a promoter of genuine happiness, and hence a positive theology of marriage and of sexuality has to be effectively communicated for people today.

To evangelise desires involves evangelising body and spirit, understanding and will, senses and affectivity. To discover Christ Jesus, son of God and son of Mary, is the key to every full human happiness. He alone is the sure Way, the complete Truth and the full Life, Christ crucified and risen. Pope John Paul, receiving the Pontifical Council for Dialogue with Non-Believers, said it in this way: "The mystery of human happiness finds its key in Jesus Christ, the archetype of every existence that gives itself."

11

IS RELIGION AN OBSTACLE TO HAPPINESS?

> People search for inner peace and harmony with themselves and with the universe. They are looking for Wisdom to guide their lives happily rather than for a Religion to belong to.
>
> Jean Vernette (French theologian)

> The number of people in possession of any criteria for discriminating between good and evil is very small; the number of the half-alive hungry for any form of spiritual experience or what offers itself as spiritual experience, high or low, good or bad, is considerable.
>
> T. S. Eliot (poet and critic)

A few decades ago there was a popular series of books to help people learn languages, with titles such as *French without Tears*. In this way, speaking a new language was presented as quite easy, really! The history of happiness is strewn with such formulas. But it is a fairly recent phenomenon to find this approach within the realm of religion. It is as if people have a desire for religion-without-tears, or more accurately, for an inner feeling that seems religious but makes no demands on the self. Instead it gives a certain peace, even a promise of depth and wisdom. But this seemingly new spirituality is far from new: it was known in the early Christian centuries as gnosticism and it has simply resurfaced in a more packaged and consumerist shape in modern times.

This do-it-yourself spirituality offers happiness with a religious label but often its incompatibility with true Christian happiness remains unrecognised. For this reason it deserves some attention in these pages, not simply to point out its dangers but to be able to appreciate the quite different happiness which is central to Christian life.

The term "New Age Movement" has been used to describe this new and complex amalgam of gnosticism and pelagianism, of astrology and superstition. It is born of genuine spiritual needs that often suffer malnutrition in the secular environment of today's culture. It thrives on the need for meaning and warmth felt by many in the anonymous deserts of urban society, where people often find themselves rootless and yet desperate for spiritual anchors.

> The interest which the New Age movement arouses is a proof that something essential is lacking within the secularised consciousness now found everywhere.
>
> Bishop Anton Schlembach (Germany)

> Paganism looks for religion in an exalted feeling of fullness here and now. Far from desacralising the world, in fact it sacralised it.
>
> Louis Pauwels (French writer)

As an umbrella term "New Age" covers a cultural tendency that goes back to the last century but has become widespread in the "developed" world in recent years. In a neutral sense it is a form of spiritual optimism, which rebels against the old dominant rationality, or "left-hand" brain, and promotes instead the values of the intuitive, the imaginative, the feminine and the holistic, or "right-hand" brain. It claims to introduce people to deeper levels of meditation, and generally to liberate them to a more creative life than is usually fostered by modern life-styles. Favourite expressions would be "spiritual wholeness" or "consciousness expansion", and as such it searches for fulfilment and happiness along paths of interiority.

Journeys within the self

"New Age" is in danger of being merely a journey in self-awareness. It has been accused of being a neo-paganism, or a contemporary version of Romanticism. That cultural movement was in part a reaction against the killing of mystery in the newly industrialised world of eighteenth-century Europe, and an implicitly religious strand was so strong in Romanticism that one of the more distinguished of recent studies of it has the title *Natural Supernaturalism,* by the American scholar, M. H. Abrams. In similar fashion the neo-paganism or neo-romanticism of the New Age movement is partly a sign of the spiritual starvation suffered by many in contemporary society. Although there are other aspects to the New Age tendency that are more obviously occultist and superstitious, here it seems best to focus on the more subtle temptation to mistake journeys of self-exploration for genuine religious happiness.

> "I have a vision, do you?" The question comes from a Brahma Kumari pamphlet. Many young people want to be pioneers in the progress towards a new humanity. Recent research in Great Britain would show that those attracted have a strong dose of idealism with at the same time the lack of a clear goal in life.
>
> Bishop Michael Fitzgerald (Pontifical Council for Interreligious Dialogue)

The oldest form of unbelief is not an intellectual rejection of God, such as became common within the last few centuries of Western thinking. Much more ancient is the biblical form of atheism known as idolatry, and at its root lies the human desire to have a tangible god that one can manage or control. Human beings seem at times to be happier with a golden calf than with the silent mystery of the true God.

One contemporary version of the golden calf is Mammon in all its crudity and complexity. But another version is more interiorised and psychologised, and therefore in tune with the privatisation of consciousness that has been mentioned more than once in these pages as a by-product of modern urban society. Even where they lack religious affiliation, many people today are rediscovering their suppressed religious needs. Indeed, precisely because they lack belonging within a church, or because they have inherited a distrust of such "institutional" forms of religion, they often look elsewhere for an answer to those real spiritual needs. Thus the happiness of faith becomes secularised, psychologised, and even commercialised, as in some forms of New Age spirituality. What is on offer there, however, is frequently a stunted happiness, devoid of revelation, seldom challenging any conversion of life, but attractive because it promises some kind of "religious experience". This is all the more alluring for people whose culture has trained them to trust only what they can experience directly.

Reductive but significant

It is relatively easy to list the reductions that lurk within this spirituality. Inner illumination replaces faith. Liberating one's creative potential replaces salvation. Prayer becomes a journey into the deep self. A vague harmony with the universe takes over from the concrete calls of social commitment. Theology is ousted by psychology or theosophy. Revelation is more in the heart than in history. Nor can such naive optimism cope with suffering, tragedy, or death.

Even if one thinks of this New Age tendency as offering a misleading form of happiness, and even if it can be diagnosed as a hidden form of unbelief, it is necessary to understand why it has become so widespread as a movement.

> The New Religious Movements often attract people who are hungry for something deeper in their religious lives. The danger is that they offer short-term good but long-term confusion. Thus people can lose their Catholic roots and in spite of temporary growth be left in a worse spiritual situation eventually.
>
> Cardinal Francis Arinze (President, Pontifical Council for Interreligious Dialogue)

> Especially during recent years, Christianity has almost been reduced to an ethical system. The creed as a doctrine of life

and source of religious or mystical experience, has been forgotten. Many are tired of this obstinate moralism and have gone to seek peace elsewhere.

Cardinal Godfried Danneels (Archbishop of Malines-Brussels)

Where such a high value is placed on the imaginative and the intuitive, the Church should not be shy to draw on her long history of symbolic expressions of faith. In 1986 a special report prepared by four dicasteries of the Holy See singled out some pastoral needs of today to which the new religious movements were responding in basically false ways: the search for belonging or community; the search for answers; the search for holism; the search for cultural identity; the need to be recognised and to be special; the search for transcendence; the need for spiritual direction; the need for vision; the need for participation and commitment. Therefore "it is important to help people realise that they are unique, loved by a personal God, with a story that is their story, and which goes from birth through death to resurrection. 'Ancient truth' has to become continually for them a 'new truth' by means of a genuine sense of renewal, but with criteria and a framework of thought that prevents them from being shaken by every novelty on their path. Special attention needs to be given to the dimension of experience, that is, to the discovery of the person of Christ through prayer and through a committed life".

Real spiritual hungers
An intellectualist answer will not meet people's expectations. Three principal hopes or desires emerge as characteristic of the more religious dimension of the search for happiness now. It looks for some experience of a spiritual kind. It gives great value to self-development. It asks to be taught practical skills of meditation and of prayer. But to crown all these, and to preserve them from going astray, a fourth practical skill should be added – the art of spiritual discernment.

Together with a situation of growing Christian illiteracy, we have an incapacity, even on the part of active Christians, to practise discernment of spirits when confronted with gnostic views of salvation. When people come to know a more intense life of faith, which may also be a questionable one, they can easily say (and it may be true): "I have never had such an experience through my Church".

Bishop Amédée Grab (Switzerland)

People need tools of judging what is true from what is false within all this contemporary emphasis on spiritual experience. Central to the exploration here has been the challenge of recognising authentic from inauthentic versions of happiness in general. The first part of this book gathered together many strands of human wisdom as to the nature of true happiness. It is not something transitory but something strong and permanent in a person's life. It is not just a matter of moods but a more anchored state of heart. It is not the result of luck but rather the outcome of a chosen response to existence. It is not on the level of pleasures only but rather of a person's whole way of life. It need not imply a situation of unclouded success but can cope with the shadows and sufferings of each life. In this way happiness goes hand in hand with the deepest layer of human freedom: it implies an option and attitude before the calls of life.

All those suggested descriptions remain within a deliberately humanist vocabulary, and yet they suggest a crucial discernment between genuine and shallow levels of understanding happiness. When one moves into a horizon of faith, the need for discernment becomes both more delicate and more guided. There is the guidance of Revelation and of the tradition of spiritual wisdom in the Church. But, as already seen, temptations to false paths become more subtle and harder to recognise at times.

Wisdom of discernment

An earlier section here touched upon the distinction that St Ignatius Loyola discovered, precisely through his own experience, between genuine consolation as something lasting, and deceptive consolation that leads to unhappiness sooner or later. This book started from the Psalmist asking "What will give us happiness?", but the happiness in question can be either short-lived, and therefore deceptive, or lasting and fruitful. By their fruits you will know them, said Jesus (Mt 7: 20). The fruits of the Spirit are unmistakeable, said St Paul, adding a verifiable list: "love, joy, peace, patience, kindness, goodness, trustfulness, gentleness and self-control" (Ga 5:22). In this light discernment might be described fairly simply as the art of judging roots in terms of lasting fruits.

More concretely still, one can suggest a series of questions to be faced whenever a person needs to discern the spiritual path he or she is taking. The overall aim is to discover whether the orientation is in tune with the values of the gospel of Christ. Positive answers to these questions indicate fidelity to Christian fundamentals. Negative answers are warnings that deception may be present and that what seems to be good now in the short-term could lead to long-term damage.

Is this leading to compassion, gentleness and self-giving or to self-concern and even to pride? This is truly a basic question. The flow of life is either towards others, especially the wounded of the world or "the least" as Jesus put it, or towards self. Involvement in some of the new spiritualities seems suspect on just this point – that what seems good for a while can be hiddenly a form of narcissism rather than a learning of love.

> Redemption is meaningless unless there is a cause for it in the actual life we live, and for the last few centuries there has been operating in our culture the secular belief that there is no such cause.
>
> Flannery O'Connor (American Catholic novelist)

> Science fiction has an enormous influence on the younger generation. They are looking for a God who includes and embraces everything. The God of the philosophers is being ousted by a new paganism.
>
> Marie-Laurent Schillinger (French sociologist)

Key questions

Is this experience leading to a stronger sense of Jesus Christ as Lord and Saviour or else is it causing a certain vagueness about God? With regard to prayer, is it rooted in a sense of reverence for God, and in a relationship of friendship with Christ, or is it content with ways of meditation that remain within a world of self-silence? Does it encourage a person to serve others in the name of justice, or is it inclined to isolation, privacy, and enjoyment of mere consciousness? Does it increase a sense of identification with the Church, and especially its sacramental life, or does it rather foster a certain alienation from the ecclesial community? Have these approaches any place for a personal Saviour, or do they tend to soft-pedal the reality of sin and evil?

If a spirituality is to be in keeping with the Christian vision, it must include the Cross. This should never mean a cult of suffering but rather a willingness to embrace the pain of love in the spirit of Christ. The Beatitudes of Jesus invite towards a vision of happiness that can include even laying down one's life for the sake of the Kingdom. Therefore a final and crucial question arises: is this New Age religiosity in danger of being too "soft" and woolly, or is it open to that slow but radical conversion of life that comes from Christian discipleship, and which is most dramatically visible through the witness of martyrs, even today? There is a depth of happiness here that is beyond humanism, and that provides a key as to how Christian faith challenges and completes the long human quest for happiness.

Such questions offer some basic tools for discernment of the trends in spirituality today. They can be neo-pagan and narcissistic. Or they can be open to the Christian vision. Even when they seem lacking in some of the Christian essentials, they can hold seeds of promise and remain open to an evangelisation of the desire that underlies them. To react against the stifling of depth in modern life-styles, to search out ways of inner stillness, to look for a spiritual wavelength worthy of humanity, to value a spirit of wonder before creation, to seek a more "holistic" and cosmic dimension of religiousness, to celebrate the physical and the symbolic, to create communities of searching for meaning – all this is admirable and good.

The danger comes only when any of these desires for happiness become stuck or stunted in some way. What starts as good ends up as less good. What began as a potential journey towards God stops short as a cult of self, or a kind of spiritual tourism, grounded in some vaguely agnostic anthropology. To avoid such a dissolving and diluting of Christian promises, it is pastorally important to identify these dubious ways of meeting the hungers of today. An immanentist and ultimately secularist approach can take over and imprison all explorations within the ego. But these needs also cry out for authentic answers from the Christian tradition. They ask for a revisiting of the great contemplatives in order to make their wisdom available for the spiritual longing of modern culture. That tradition is one rooted in a happiness of a very different kind than the easy self-fulfilment of secular images. It is to that difference that we can now turn.

12

THE BEATITUDES OF THE GOSPEL

Certainly, beatitude is yet to come, but why cannot our happiness be a way towards it?

Cardinal François Marty (formerly Archbishop of Paris)

While you are proclaiming peace with your lips, be careful to have it even more fully in your heart.

St Francis of Assisi

It is time to come to the heart of the gospels, to the proclamation by Jesus of his vision of happiness. The Beatitudes come at the opening of his preaching, at the start of what is known as the Sermon on the Mount in St Matthew's Gospel (5:1-12). Needless to say this is far from being the only gospel passage concerning happiness. At the birth of Jesus the message to the shepherds was one of great joy. From the outset of Christ's preaching his proclamation was of Good News. In the parable of the Last Judgment, the invitation is to join in the Lord's happiness. At his Last Supper Jesus promised that his joy would make ours complete. But down through the ages, the Beatitudes have been seen as the keystone of a Christian version of happiness. This extraordinary set of sayings has been viewed as the charter of Christianity, the foundation of its civilisation of love.

Volumes have been written on the Beatitudes – by experts in scripture, by authors of spiritual reflections, even by unbelieving philosophers. In theology through the centuries the importance of these statements has seemed transparent to all. They praise a set of personal attitudes. They stress inner dispositions of heart. They celebrate a happiness that is both present and future. Thus these words of Jesus are both a recognition of a happiness in people now and a promise of its reward and fulfilment beyond this world.

Beatitudes as autobiographical

As Pope John Paul II expressed it, speaking to a huge gathering of young people on Palm Sunday 1991, Christ himself is "the living incarnation of the eight Beatitudes. He knows their entire truth". Whatever else one may come to realise about the Beatitudes, it helps to begin by realising that they are autobiographical. They were lived at their most transparent in the person of Jesus himself. It is worth recalling that Jesus did choose a way of life. At the core of the mysterious event described in the gospels as his "temptation in the desert" lies a struggle of attitudes between immediate satisfaction and a deeper trust in the word of God. The three areas where those gospel temptations attacked the humanity of Jesus are in fact three perennial areas of temptation to unbelief. It can come through "bread", or any of the hungers of the body. It can come through desire for power and success, as in the temptation to the "kingdoms of the earth". Or, even more subtly, temptation can come within the motivations of the human heart, and it is a question of pride, of trusting oneself so much that one can throw oneself off a "high temple". Deceptive happiness comes from giving in to those three temptations, in their myriad disguises. A more lasting and genuine happiness comes from ordering one's life according to the word of God and rooting one's trust in God alone. Then the other things fall into place. It is the isolation of bread, or of kingdoms, or of human enterprises, that makes happiness false and idolatrous.

In this light, Jesus in the desert rejected deceptive forms of happiness and false roads to being the saviour. Hence the opening of the Sermon on the Mount is even more personal. It announces the way of true happiness that Jesus has chosen through struggle. Another passage of Scripture says that Jesus was a man like us in all things but sin (Heb 4:15). Earlier in this book it was shown how the struggle of false against true happiness goes on in every heart and in every culture. Now one can recognise that drama as a continuation of the temptations of Jesus himself. It is significant that Jesus emerges from that desert struggle with a proclamation of happiness in the shape of his Beatitudes.

A beatitude is an exclamation of congratulations that recognises an existing state of happiness.

Benedict Viviano (Dominican scripture scholar)

A Francis of Assisi can make you understand the joy within poverty. Preaching on its own will not do so.

Cardinal Godfried Danneels (Archbishop of Malines-Brussels)

Everybody would agree that the values embodied in the Beatitudes challenge the complacent assumptions about happiness that dominate our world and have always done so. It is not only within the images of today's world of advertising that one finds a happiness being promoted that seems directly in contradiction to these sentences in the gospel. But those counter-beatitudes are stark today. The message is imaged everywhere. Happy are the moneyed ones – they can buy all they want. Happy are the tough people – they will get their way. Happy are those who create a good impression – they shall be universally admired. And so on. Does this mean that the happiness proposed by Christ is totally contrary to human happiness? Some interpretations take that line and stress the opposition between these ideals and the natural view of happiness.

Evangelising human happiness

We have to offer a critique of happiness from the viewpoint of beatitude.

Jacques Ellul (French Protestant theologian)

It seems wiser to see the Beatitudes of Christ in total opposition only to superficial and egoist versions of happiness, but in profound harmony with the happiness that is the authentic goal of human desire. Pastorally, it seems most helpful to present the Beatitudes as the liberation of natural happiness into new depth. In this way the powerful statements of Christ invite us away from mere silliness, and beyond common sense, and towards a fuller freedom and joy rooted in another set of attitudes. Ultimately the Beatitudes are rooted in a conversion of heart to the values of Christ's self-giving love.

Certainly the Beatitudes question the more shallow approaches to happiness but they lead towards a fuller truth about humanity. They shatter conventional assumptions about happiness which have always dominated the secular world, whether in the time of Jesus or now. Their truth is challenging and even paradoxical, but far from being beyond our grasp, it is in fact verifiable within our human experience. This vision comes to guide a person's life only as the fruit of an evangelisation of one's desires. It is born from a conversion to the values of the heart of Christ. Since that conversion is at its most powerful in the saints, this liberated happiness shows most transparently in the witness of their lives, as has already been touched upon in chapter 5.

How can one best describe this crowning freedom of happiness that is expressed in the Beatitudes? These sentences point to a way of life that is rooted in love and self-surrender. They point to a personal option that goes completely beyond egoism and self-security. It transforms the agenda of happiness totally and reveals a surprising joy in an alternative set of attitudes, especially towards the poor and wounded of the world: these attitudes include a vulnerability that lets go of self-importance, a spirit of gentleness, a compassion with those in pain, a courage in the service of the weak, a forgiveness towards all, a simplicity of heart, a capacity to heal divisions, and the ultimate freedom of suffering happily for the sake of right.

Summary of Christian happiness

These qualities add up to a new heart and a new happiness. They are utterly concrete and incarnate, even though to our unconverted selves they can seem distant and idealist. But these qualities are the essential marks of the full Christian life. They were totally lived in Christ himself. They have been often transparent in the humanity of saints whether canonised or unknown. They are a summary of Christian happiness and the happiness which they promise is simply the fruit of living out Christ's way of love.

> Since Christ is the only one who has God's happiness as his own he is the only one who can save and make happy every human being.
>> Tibor Horváth (Hungarian-Canadian theologian)

> The Beatitudes incorporate certain dispositions for ministry, challenging characteristics of what it is to be a disciple of Jesus. but they also include the promise of resurrection.
>> Max Oliva (American writer)

Seen in this way, these extraordinary words of Jesus can furnish a real bridge for dialogue between believers and non-believers on the topic of happiness. The non-believer may not be able to receive these words as revelation but this need not block a recognition of their power and indeed of their human truth. Is it not true that a deeper joy is experienced whenever someone risks reaching out beyond the conventional shields of selfishness? Is it not true that those who dedicate themselves in practice to solidarity with the poor or to work of reconciliation experience something of the joy of which the Beatitudes speak? Is it not true that a greater happiness results from tenderness than from arrogance? Far from being purely spiritual in a narrow sense, these promises are verified in ordinary human reality. Moreover, this truth is available to believers and non-believers alike as a marvellous starting-point for dialogue.

Certainly there are dimensions to the Beatitudes that can only be grasped in faith. In particular nearly all the promises of reward point to a future that is not of this world. In St Luke's version of the Beatitudes this element of future promise and warning is even stronger. This eschatological horizon in fact leads towards the next chapter here, which will deal with the question of eternal happiness. The beatitudes, however, summarise the deep values lived by

Christ himself and which are echoed in human experience, whenever happiness is the outcome of a genuine Christian conversion to generosity and freedom of heart. In this sense, far from being the opposite of human happiness, they are its liberation, and far from being irrelevant to human history, they offer the foundation for a civilisation of love.

13

PROMISE OF ETERNAL HAPPINESS

God has made us for Beatitude – and we go searching, in an impoverished way, for happiness. Happiness is what we conceive and desire spontaneously. It is something unworthy of us, and which the deepest part of our nature rejects. Beatitude is God. The Christian does not expect happiness. He expects the new heavens and the new earth. Happiness is all that and can be only that.

Henri de Lubac (French theologian and cardinal)

The sense of *eternal* happiness seems to be in trouble in today's culture, even for many believers. If the word "happiness" itself can have reductive connotations, this certainly makes any connection between happiness and eternity problematic. But perhaps the most common difficulties come from people's images of eternity.

A medieval parable

In popular consciousness the notion of eternal happiness can often evoke something vague and boring. Childish pictures of sitting around singing hymns with thousands of angels do not seem very attractive! In this respect there is a delightful medieval legend about a monk who found it hard to believe in eternal happiness as attractive. To him it seemed like something going on and on for ever in a monotonous way. While troubled with these questions, he wandered into a forest one day and heard the song of a nightingale. He stopped to enjoy the beauty of it, and stayed there a long time, absorbed. When he returned to his monastery, everything had changed. Nobody knew him. He gave them the name of the abbot and was told that this famous abbot was dead about a thousand years! This old tale is a simple parable that points to the incomprehensible fullness of eternal happiness. It is like those moments in life when time stands still, when the heart is overwhelmed with wonder, or when the beauty of creation offers, so to speak, a glimpse of glory. The monk in that tale learned that eternity is literally timeless.

But difficulties about eternity run deeper in today's secularised world and show themselves in many ways. There seems to be a general blindspot in modern culture to any version of happiness that goes beyond this present world. Perhaps most people do not think things out rationally or reflectively. Instead they live within the symbolic universe that their culture offers them, and whose assumptions they move within almost like the air they breathe. In this respect one of the key features of contemporary culture is its absolutising of the immanent. When taken together with liberal assumptions about human autonomy, it is easy to see that any traditional sense of after-life or of eternal happiness is not so much denied as untrue as rendered unreal and hence incredible for many people today. A more militant age of unbelief was inclined to dismiss eternity as an illusion, even a dangerous distraction from the tasks of human history, but nowadays eternal life is not argued about. Instead it is marginalised silently into something remote and intangible.

Eclipse of a sense of eternity

> The Christian promise of eternal happiness with God appears to people as a divine recompense for the lack of earthly happiness. They accept this promise as the terminus of their trying to live in Christ.
>
> Bishop M'Sanda Tsinda Hata (Zaire)

> Living here and now as Christians of hope, we need not make "heaven" the total opposite of "earth"; rather we can look on it as the end of a process of maturing and of giving birth.
>
> Gustave Martelet (French theologian)

Moreover, a diminishing of the sense of eternal happiness is not uncommon even among believers today. It may be sometimes avoided on the grounds that it could be an escapist consolation. Again, some believers may envisage happiness beyond the grave in rather inadequate ways, for instance as a balancing of accounts: somehow the sacrifices of this life will be made worthwhile in another life. In practice, perhaps it is only when there is some closeness of death that eternity becomes a real question. In ordinary times, people are preoccupied by immediacies. They may have a good level of commitment and of prayer, and they may experience their faith as inviting them to lives of love, but that love, however admirable and deep, is often understood in terms of this life only.

Among people of less religious formation, a version of Christianity is still widespread that sees eternal happiness as a childish and simplistic compensation for the pains and troubles of this life. There are many whose faith is restricted to a language of obligation and ritual, and who go through their lives with immature notions of religion, sadly ignorant of the full range of the gospel as gift and as challenge.

Saint Paul

> Why, alas, is everything infinite except our happiness? The longing for true love is infinite but our happiness is finite.
>
> Goethe

> This is the first inkling of eternity – to have time for love.
>
> Rainer Maria Rilke

There is then a real pastoral need for a renewal of the sense of eternal happiness within people's faith language and spirituality today. But how can this best be helped? In one sense this problem is part of the human condition. It has always been hard to find the right language for this central hope of faith. One remembers St Paul's famous words about it: "The things that no eye has seen and no ear

has heard, things beyond the mind of man, all that God has prepared for those who love him" (1 Co 2:9). Yet later in that same
letter St Paul is quite emphatic about the truth of resurrection and
eternal life: "If our hope in Christ has been for this life only, we
are the most unfortunate of all people" (1 Co 15:19). On the one
hand a healthy shyness is essential before the inexpressible. On the
other hand one has to communicate the full Christian promise of
life and of happiness as going beyond death into resurrection and
eternity.

> What Christ does is to expand our desires rather than teach
> us to contain them.
>
> Michael Mason (Australian writer)

> This "already" is further strengthened by the "not yet". . .
> And this "not yet" invites us to action, to creativity, to use
> all the powers of our imagination, of our will and heart.
> With this "not yet" our age is an open age.
>
> Franc Rodé (Slovenian theologian)

It is vital to avoid dichotomising "earth" and "eternity" in a way
that it does small justice to the richness of the Christian vision. It
should not be a question of opting for one *or* other as forms of
happiness. Rather there is one flow of life through the incomprehensible barrier of death into the unimaginable gift of eternity.
Thus it is not a matter of rival or competing forms of happiness but
rather of fullness of life in two ways. There is both continuity and
discontinuity between what Aquinas, as was mentioned, called
imperfect and perfect happiness.

What can help towards a more adequate and positive presentation of eternal happiness? Negatively many inadequate images
need to be set aside before people can realise that heaven is less a
place than a state of being-with-God face to face.

Fullness of love

Any more authentic catechesis on eternity will be centred on
Christ and be couched in terms of love. The key to a specifically

Christian vision of eternity is a sharing in the glory of the Risen Christ. That death is not the end of everything is at the heart of the Good News. Indeed, ordinary struggling life can be re-read in the light of Christ's death and resurrection and of the promise of everlasting life. With Christ all the everyday dyings of self-giving become minor gateways into happiness, and this in turn offers a foretaste of the more mysterious passover with Christ through death into a different life.

> The sense of mystery is growing. The Church must return to a more explicit proclamation of mystery.
> Nikolaus Lobkowicz (German theologian)

> Beatitude is a state where we no longer seek the good but rest in its possession.
> Frederick Crowe (Canadian theologian)

Finally, it is worth recalling that for St Thomas Aquinas there were two forms of human love, a love of striving and desiring, and a love of resting and enjoying. One wavelength of love is active and energetic in its desire. The other is passive and receptive in its joy. The first is typical of the search for happiness in this life. The second is more characteristic of its fulfilment in eternity. Thus the language of struggle which is familiar and normal in the pursuit of happiness here in this world is not the language that will best help us to understand the nature of the happiness that awaits us in eternity. And yet, even in this world – as in the example of the medieval parable referred to earlier – there are many experiences that touch on this more contemplative capacity for joy within everybody. It is on the basis of such wonder and love, which basks in a sense of presence and gratitude, that one can best approach the transcendent reality of eternal happiness. In this sense it is in continuity with what people know of happiness in this life.But it is also different and discontinuous. The happiness of eternity is beyond our language. There are few religious realities to which a famous teaching of the Fourth Lateran Council is more applicable:

it held that in matters of God our speaking in human comparisons is always more inadequate than adequate. But of one thing one can be sure in faith: this happiness, the nature of which cannot be fully understood or expressed, is promised as a gift by God, and it will be the final fulfilment of all human hopes and searchings.

A total happiness

> I believe that already in this world we can participate, through a mysterious language, in what is incorruptible and infinite.
>
> Françoise Dolto (French writer)

> Without the mystery of the Cross, all our thinking about happiness can remain merely utopian.
>
> Bishop Joseph Rodericks (India)

Again Aquinas is beautifully blunt about it: happiness must mean having everything. But people today are seldom in touch with this huge hunger for everything, and because of this impoverishment, the notion of eternity is eclipsed for them. At the Plenary Assembly, Cardinal Danneels argued forcefully that people today need to be liberated from a constricting smallness in their own desires and to be told "you are much greater than you think".

There are many ways of making sense of eternal happiness, but essentially one has to turn to the person of Christ. Our final happiness will be his happiness. His happiness will be shared with us. That sharing is true here in this life, as was seen in the previous chapter on the Beatitudes. It is true in a more complete way in eternity, even though that way remains beyond our best images and words. Here one can speak, even eloquently, about the happiness of God as made transparent in Jesus Christ. Yes, indeed, God is happiness because God is love. But there remains a constant barrier between our words and the mystery we gesture towards in the words. Only in faith can we trust that in eternity we shall understand this happiness of God and enjoy a vision face to face. It is through Christ that we know this invitation to all of humanity to share the happiness of God, both here and hereafter. "There we will see, we will love, and we will praise without end" (St Augustine, *The City of God*).

14

PASTORAL APPROACHES TO HAPPINESS

The Church is a source of joy, of every kind of joy intended
for this world. What you have done against the Church, you
have done against joy.

Georges Bernanos (French novelist)

On the threshold of the third millennium, the Spirit is
preparing a huge vision for us. We all have a great mission.
We need women and men of prayer and action. We need
contemplation and courage.

Josef Zverina (Czech theologian)

From everything that has been said in previous chapters, it is obvious that the issue of happiness is a crucial one for the contemporary world, that it touches on many of the challenges of our time,
and that it provides an excellent agenda for dialogue between
believers and non-believers. It has also become clear that the
theme of happiness is not only at the centre of human desire but at
the centre of God's revelation in Christ. Indeed that coincidence is
no accident: it is the loving plan of creation that the search for happiness should be crowned by the gift of happiness from God both
here and hereafter.

Hence a ministry of happiness is a vital element in evangelisation, that evangelisation which is the core of the Church's mission
always. Was not the first preaching of Jesus a proclamation of happiness? "The time has come", he said, "and the kingdom of God is
close at hand. Repent, and believe the Good News" (Mk 1:15). He
announced an urgent happiness because even then it required conversion of heart before it could be recognised. Thus the Church's
ministry of happiness involves two tasks: a wise critique of what is
damaging or illusory in the images of happiness today, and a
renewed invitation to discover the new happiness revealed in Jesus
Christ.

Paradoxically, real happiness requires a self-sacrificing love which often appears to ask the sacrifice of the more immediate happiness we want. In this sense the search for happiness is marked by the paschal rhythm of dying and rising.

> A "miracle" of the Gospel is its capacity to be forever open to different cultures, in the sense of being lived fully and of accepting the culture at the same time as purifying it of whatever may be dehumanising.
>
> Bishop Ramón Echarren Ystúriz (Canary Islands)

> Christianity would never have gone beyond the frontiers of Palestine, if it had not been, in its essence, a promise of happiness, a promise of joy offered to humanity.
>
> Franc Rodé (Slovenian theologian)

In brief, the pastoral task entails a "no" and a "yes", but it is important that the liberating "yes" be not drowned by the necessary "no". Urgent though it may be to expose the ills of our world, it is even more urgent to communicate Christ as Good News for this moment in history. How is this to be done? It is the aim of this concluding section to gather together various positive suggestions in this regard.

A gathering of pastoral insights

It is part of the huge adventure of Church history that different cultures and different epochs always require a new communication of the Good News of Christ. Otherwise the deep happiness that comes from faith can remain sadly unknown to new generations. If younger people, in particular, encounter only a language of faith that does not seem to embody happiness, or does not invite them to growth into new happiness, then they will often remain disappointed and at a distance from Christianity. Young people are in danger of seeing the Church only as it is presented in the media – as "a rule-making institution rather than a community of searching believers" – to cite a commonplace or stereotype. Or, in the words of an Irish bishop, "the Church is seen as an organisation rather than as a family". To counter this unhappy image they need to experience a Church of hope, a Church that embraces human realities and discerns what is positive in today's world. This will come about especially through an active togetherness and through a witness of faith lived in communion with others with contagious joy.

> Sin is the progressive limitation of existence to an attainable "now" instead of the unlimited newness of tomorrow.
>
> Tibor Horváth (Hungarian-Canadian theologian)

Living the faith with contagious joy

The core of happiness is simple and perennial: it is to love and to be loved. But this reality is often lost sight of in the pressures and distractions of modern living. The overload of images and of information tends to relativise everything and leave people grasping at only transitory forms of happiness. Christian faith has the great answer to all this searching – indeed God's own answer in Christ – but in practice believers have to witness to that faith with honesty and authenticity.

The core of evangelisation is: "God loves you, Christ came for you". The Church preaches this God who has loved us so much that the Son became flesh for us. He is God who draws close to us, who communicates with us, who joins himself with us, the true Emmanuel. This communion has been promised by the Lord not simply for this life, but above all as a victory over sin and death through sharing in his resurrection, and as face-to-face friendship with God for ever. Without this hope of eternal life, where all pains and evils are overcome, the human person is seriously mutilated: "proclamation of this joy must never be lacking in the new evangelisation" (Synod of European Bishops, 14 December 1991).

The particular culture to which faith must speak today is more impressed by experience than by ideas. In this sense Cardinal Paulos Tzadua of *Ethiopia* recalled the celebrated statement by Pope Paul VI that people today listen "more willingly to witnesses than to teachers" *(Evangelii nuntiandi, 41)*.

Words alone are weak, but the world is hungry for symbols or parables. It needs a liturgy that is genuinely a celebration. It needs a preaching that is more imaginative and intuitive – like that of Jesus himself. Most of all, it needs ordinary saints whose humanity makes Christian happiness visible, incarnate and contagious.

A comment from **Holland** insisted that to communicate a faith that claims to offer genuine happiness, it is important to touch people's hopes and show that the gospel is in tune with their full humanity. In similar terms a report from **Australia** stressed that although Christianity has to challenge the falsities of contemporary culture, with all its radical immanentism, much depends on how that critique is expressed. The people who live within a given set of assumptions need to hear their positive values affirmed before being ready to discern the negative aspects also there. It is another version of putting "yes" before "no", as mentioned at the outset of this chapter.

Happiness and justice

> The service of social justice is appealing for many non-believers, and may help them to come to religion.
>
> Bishop Paul Shan (Taiwan)

From **Taiwan** and from **Angola** came reminders of the social dimension of any ministry of Christian happiness. This happiness is not merely personal in a narrow sense. It is Good News for entire peoples. The stance of Christians over issues of justice is one of the ways in which faith is given credibility in today's sceptical Western world, and it is also one of the ways in which Christian happiness is best embodied in situations of great social suffering. From **Kenya** came claims that in such non-individualist cultures as exist in Africa, the social message of the gospels "fits" the mentality of the people and gives depth to their natural sense of solidarity.

From **Brazil** it was pointed out that the communication of Christian faith as genuine happiness in fact entails a whole new evangelisation in depth. An impoverished level of Christian commitment results in the banishing of the power of faith to the margins of existence. Nominal Christians "use" the Church as a pleasant icing on the cake of a bourgeois existence, it was said. For them to know the happiness offered by the Gospel would mean that new evangelisation which Pope John Paul has never tired of proposing with urgency. The happiness offered by the gospels goes beyond any vaguely religious humanism: it is the happiness of the Beatitudes. In this way the Good News of Christ involves both a continuity and a discontinuity with "normal" happiness. In short, true happiness is born from a conversion away from the false images of happiness that dominate much of our contemporary culture.

Many difficulties connected with happiness in the First World also concern the understanding of freedom. The emphasis can fall so much on freedom "from" that the older freedom "for" becomes forgotten or at least secondary. If so, a merely egoist version of liberation can oust goals of generosity and responsibility. The people of God need to be helped renew that older and deeper freedom: if they can realise that faith is not a limitation but rather a commitment for a larger freedom, then they rediscover hope. When such a vision of hope comes alive, people find a new and happy energy in their faith and in their church belonging.

Happiness in practice

In the long term facing the truth is the only way to lasting happiness.

Peter Hodgson (English scientist)

Christianity has to be presented, not in terms of a message, but as an event, as something that truly happened in time and space and continues to happen today. If this calls us to a new evangelisation, it is because our situation is not very healthy.

Bishop Francisco Javier Martínez (Spain)

But how is all this to be achieved pastorally? It is not enough to lament the distortions. It is not enough to offer a clear exposition in intellectual terms. As already seen, the tendency of contemporary culture is to be "put off" by the merely conceptual and to seek the experiential. It is often in their hearts or dispositions that people are imprisoned. If so, they will be reached only by something that speaks to hearts and invites them to something of new experience and something of fuller freedom.

In so far as the shaping culture is alien and unChristian, any evangelising of desires has to involve some element of rupture with current assumptions about happiness. It has to expose the impoverishment of the subjective stance, and it has to open people up to a different vision of fulfilment through the person and values of Jesus Christ rather than through self-satisfaction. Faith is much more in need of personal and mature conviction today than previously, and such a faith is served by a solid proclamation of the gospel in all its doctrinal and existential aspects.

A contribution from **Canada** stressed the need to identify "key experiences" within people's lives and to give them opportunities to move from these into attitudes of prayer. People are often trapped within passivities and need to discover their own hungers and hopes. They also need to move from a nominal religion to an encounter with the power of revelation. This journey of growth can offer a most fruitful deepening of faith and an entry into a new happiness as a more mature Christian. In fact another Canadian comment praised the model of conversion embodied in the twelve steps of Alcoholics Anonymous. It hinges on an admission of powerlessness and the need for a "higher power" to help a person escape from addiction. Apart from its proved success in practice, this process also casts light on the struggle needed to discover and live a specifically Christian happiness. It is a process of death and resurrection, and involves dying to egoist forms of happiness in order to enter into the joy of new life with Christ.

Starting from experience
In very similar terms a contribution from **Spain** argued that when

suitable ways of evangelisation are found, the fruits of the gospel
are as fresh as they have always been, and even for young people
who seem stuck within secularised attitudes. What is needed is a
pastoral approach that evokes a basic religious sense, something
that is often missing in young people now. When the attraction of
the person of Christ is experienced – not as message but as
encounter – there results a liberating sense of surprise, of thanksgiving, of freedom and of joy. Moreover, a renewed sense of
Church also emerges as equally a source of happiness, and not as a
distant institution.

> The pedagogy of sainthood needs to root itself on the princi-
> ple that one cannot separate the issue of eternal happiness
> from questions of social and personal happiness.
>
> Józef Majka (Polish theologian)

> The Church has to proclaim clearly that only when one has
> accepted the full message of the Gospels is it possible to
> have a genuine happiness already in this world.
>
> Archbishop Antonio Moreno (Chile)

In this process of a new evangelisation a special gift of the Church,
today as always, lies in a community, genuinely rooted in faith,
hope and love. Where secularisation tends to isolate people spiritually, from the beginning, Christianity – as recorded in the Acts of
the Apostles – grew through communities who shared and lived
the happiness of Christ. Where secularisation makes relationships
fragile and keeps prayer cut off in an impotent privacy, believers
have to build up communities of true Christian freedom, where
prayer is the source of life. Happiness then comes from that listening where the heart is spoken to by God. Prayer transforms a person's life through a dialogue of faith and of love with the God who
is the source of all happiness, personal and social. If this becomes
real, there is little danger of a damaging opposition between Christian happiness here and hereafter. "These remained faithful to the
teaching of the apostles, to the brotherhood, to the breaking of

bread and to the prayers" (Acts 2:42). With these pillars of growth in faith, the door is open to a living happiness in tune with the gospel. Then Christians become a positive invitation to non-believers to wonder about the source of such visible and lived happiness (Acts 4:33). Where these evangelical conditions come alive, happiness is the fruit given by the Lord, and a fruit that in turn becomes a powerful instrument of evangelisation: "They praised God and were looked up to by everyone. Day by day the Lord added to their community those destined to be saved" (Acts, 2:47).

A converted happiness

> Jesus did not seek for happiness. Neither did he seek for suffering and the cross. He received them . . . Happiness is given as a plus to those who choose life.
> Cardinal Albert Decourtray (Archbishop of Lyons)

It would be wrong to present the Gospel just as an invitation to happiness. At the heart of revelation is a gift of God, a salvation in Christ that brings new happiness into the world. Christianity is not primarily a search for happiness but rather a conversion to a gift and to a way of love. Certainly that discovery and that commitment lead to happiness – but indirectly, as a fruit rather than as a goal.

Is the quest for happiness to be equated with the quest for meaning? Perhaps this often seems true within the horizons of the First World. But if one looks at the whole planet, the vast majority of people need something else. Somehow their reality of suffering and impoverishment has to be integrated into a Christian understanding of happiness.

At the beginning and end of John's Gospel the signs of the presence of Jesus as Saviour come in parallel moments of fullness. At the wedding of Cana the sign is of abundance of wine. At the lakeside of Tiberias the sign is of abundance of fish. In both episodes the gift of fullness comes after some experience of human failure or emptiness. Something of the same pattern will always be true of

Christian happiness. It cannot forget failure, suffering and sin. It cannot think of itself as ever complete in this life. Above all, it is ultimately a grace from God, the fruit of his liberation of our hearts for fullness of life and of love.

The world of non-belief is one that has many shades and tones today. The topic of happiness has proved an excellent one as a basis for discerning some of the central struggles of meaning and value, as well as of faith and non-belief. Above all it has been a topic that fits the "road" that is humanity. In his first encyclical Pope John Paul II stressed that humankind "is the primary and fundamental way for the Church". In Christ that road leads to God and announces a happiness that is ultimately the happiness of God.

The secret of God

> The test of all happiness is gratitude.
>
> G. K. Chesterton (English Catholic writer)

In the closing pages of *Orthodoxy*, G. K. Chesterton offers a uniquely eloquent treatment of Christian happiness. First published in 1908, this book comes back again and again to happiness as both a hallmark of faith and ultimately as a glimpse of God. Linking happiness essentially with a sense of thanksgiving, he adds that where happiness goes wrong, it is when it becomes "proud and prosperous". In his view, it is part of the "eternal revolution" of Christianity to cultivate a healthy "suspicion" about this complacent happiness, which is always incapable of coping with the mixture of joy and sorrow that is human existence. In Chesterton's vision when human beings are fully alive "joy is the fundamental thing" and grief the "superficial" reality. But he goes further: he links this with Christian faith where "joy becomes something gigantic and sadness something special and small". His final paragraph, in an imaginative leap, celebrates this "secret of the Christian" as the secret of Christ himself. It is as if "there was some one thing that was too great for God to show us when he walked upon our earth" – the "mirth" or happiness in the heart of

Christ.

This present book has also been written in the conviction that happiness is utterly human and yet larger than human. Jesus did not proclaim a magic formula for happiness. The Gospel tells of the secret of a mysterious happiness which is like a treasure hidden in a field. Whoever discovers this happiness, goes away with the freedom to let go of everything in order to own this treasure offered to everyone.

Happiness has offered a fertile topic for dialogue with non-believers, because it is such a fundamental reality in human experience and because it links up with such basic needs of people: "the future of humanity lies in the hands of those who are strong enough to provide coming generations with reasons for living and hoping" (*Gaudium et spes,* 31). To create that future will involve an evangelisation of our hearts' desires, and an opening of the way to Christ, in keeping with his words that "my own joy may be in you and your joy be complete" (Jn 15:11).

CONCLUSION

1. Universal aspiration to happiness

Every person without exception wants to be happy. And all of human unhappiness comes from the fact that people go astray in their search for happiness. Already, four centuries before Jesus Christ, the philosopher Aristotle affirmed: "There is no doubt that the last end of mankind is happiness. But some locate it in riches, others in pleasure, others in power, others still in a virtuous life". "Love but take care over what you love", said St Augustine. And Bossuet added: "The whole aim of humanity is to be happy. To place happiness where it should be is the source of every good. And the source of all evil is to place it where it should not be".

2. Evangelisation of desire

The aspiration to happiness is universal. It expresses itself equally in the wisdom of popular sayings as in that of philosophers. It pervades cultures. It inspires literature and art, laws and education. It is the spur of nations. It is the heart of religions. Everywhere the desire for it asserts its fullness, its duration, its intensity and its harmony.

Traditional civilisations mirror themselves in the personal and family happiness sung about in Psalms, the gift of life of earthly goods, as well as their transitory nature, and the final security that comes from God as the source of all good.

These cultures are often threatened by the shock of modernity. Other models of happiness flaunt themselves, whose immediacy fascinates and tends to marginalise religion, which is seen as no longer useful to satisfy daily needs.

The collapse of the atheist ideology of marxist-leninism is an earth-shaking event, whose shock waves are having major effects throughout the world. The tragic failure of this false and worldly messianism, a veritable Chernobyl of souls, has brought about a great spiritual void. But leaving the desert does not mean entering the Promised Land. From the facile identification of happiness and freedom, disillusions are born. A new myth of an earthly paradise asserts itself through the frenetic pursuit of pleasure, of wealth, of power. The return of religiousness goes hand in hand with the return of idols. It calls for true witnesses of the God of Love and of Light; those very men and women, who were yesterday indomitable in their rejection of hate and of lies, today have to be transparent and radiant in their profession of faith in the living God.

The cultures of modernity ally themselves to the paganisms of antiquity, and are rediscovering its familiar oscillations between immediate happiness and deep despair. New versions of epicurean and stoic wisdom are asserting themselves. A return of gnosticism promises happiness through knowledge. These metamorphoses of happiness call forth a new proclamation of the gospel of happiness by means of an evangelisation of desires.

3. The mysterious happiness of the Gospel

Jesus did not come to give us a magic recipe for certain happiness. The Gospel shares with us the secret of a mysterious happiness akin to the treasure hidden in a field. And he who discovers it goes away, sells all he possesses and buys it. The apostle Peter offers this recommendation: "Keep your eyes fixed on the face of the Lord, 'as a lamp for lighting a way through the dark until the dawn comes and the morning star rises in your minds' " (2 P 1:19).

"Show us the Father and that will suffice", said the Jews to Jesus. Or again "Where do you live?" *"Come and see"*, he answered them. Our contemporaries put the same question to us. The Christ of the Beatitudes answers our deep needs, which often need to be awoken where sensibilities have been dulled. Too many Christians seem to live as if God did not exist. And because of this the presence of God lacks public visibility in secularised societies. Dialogue between Christians and non-believers certainly needs research and analysis, reflections and proposals. But it does not reduce itself to that.

Just as much as their ancestors, people today need God. If those who adore the true God do not make him known and do not share the happiness of living in his presence and of loving every person as his children, then there are other messengers to make themselves heard, and other images which draw people, other practices that become common, and other forms of unhappiness which imprison humanity in the lonely and the finite.

4. Christians, people of faith, messengers of hope, sowers of love
We are beings created for love. Indeed, nobody can live without loving and being loved. And true happiness is in God. Moreover, the dialogue between Christians and non-believers is one that roots itself in prayer, nourishes itself in contemplation and in the grace of the sacraments, and is shared in ecclesial communities of faith, hope and love. Christianity is a happiness which radiates in Love by means of gift and pardon. "There is more joy in giving than in receiving", said Jesus. He said it and he showed it, by his life and by his death, his blessed passion and his glorious resurrection.

"All of us without exception want to be happy". And in his Confessions St Augustine adds: "Happiness of life, Lord, is to experience love for you, from you, because of you. The happy life is one born of truth. It means joy born from you who are the truth, my God, my light. The joy of truth is what everyone desires".

The call of the Christian is to share this generously on the different roads travelled by humanity today, roads that are new and sometimes dangerous, but always open to people on the move, *homo viator*, from time to eternity, in search of happiness, happy to meet Jesus on the way as a companion of Emmaus. "And they recognised him in the breaking of bread", bread shared, love divided out, and already on this eucharistic earth, a touch of Paradise, the final home of happiness, where "there will be no more death. and no more mourning or sadness. The world of the Past has gone. I am making the whole creation new" (Rv 21: 4-5).

In dialogue with non-believers, the Christian who witnesses to his faith in Christ is a messenger of hope and a sower of love.

"The future is in the hands of those who can give tomorrow's generations reasons to live and to hope" (Vatican II, *Gaudium et spes*, 31).

EPILOGUE

HUNGER FOR TRUE HAPPINESS

(The text of the introductory discourse by Cardinal Poupard, presenting the participants of the Plenary Assembly of the Pontifical Council for Dialogue with Non-Believers to Pope John Paul II on 18 March 1991)

Vivere omnes beate volunt. Thus began the treatise *De Vita Beata* dedicated by Seneca to his brother Gallio.

Every person tries to be happy. There are no exceptions. Even if they employ different means, they are seeking the same goal. This is the motive behind everyone's actions, including those on the way to perdition". Thus Pascal claims in a celebrated passage of his *Pensées.*

In similar fashion the Pontifical Council for Dialogue with Non-Believers chose this longing for happiness, which is at the heart of human history even if shadowed by unhappiness, as its theme for reflection and dialogue with non-believers.

Makarioi, Blessed, Jesus tells us in the Gospel, this Good News for humankind in quest of happiness, although surrounded by constant trials that are always taking new shape and new life.

Christus, Solutio omnium difficultatum, affirms St Augustine. For too many of our contemporaries, Christianity is only a problem, whereas it opens wide the door on the luminous mystery of him who is *the Way, the Truth, the Life.*

This is the challenge for the Church in dialogue with those who are non-believing, indifferent or agnostic, to find the suitable means to share with them in a warm and convincing way the grace of faith in Christ, the endless source of happiness and joy.

Our *Plenaria* has highlighted the picture of humankind today, with all its contrasts, from material wealth to spiritual poverty, from economic poverty to spiritual hunger, in a diversity of cultures and of socio-political situations. Atheistic regimes have fall-en, and suddenly a number of obstacles have disappeared, which blocked the light of Truth from reaching minds and the joy of believing from expanding hearts. But equally opaque barriers con-tinue to block the road: a widespread atheism, more practical then theoretical, a tranquil agnosticism, a disenchanted scepticism, a self-indulgent hedonism, a gross materialism.

But the thirst for true happiness, for certain truth, for moral rec-titude, which has never been absent from humanity, is making headway again along different paths, which it is the duty of the Church to discover, in order to travel those ways without fear, with the charity of the Good Shepherd on all the roads to Emmaus.

Tirelessly, Most Holy Father, you travel all these ways of humanity along the routes of the world, as an indefatigable mes-senger of the Church, this House of Happiness which opens wide its doors to all people and helps them to discover that intensity of pleasure is not enough to meet the thirst for happiness, and that desire is never satisfied until it allows itself be grasped by the Joy that comes from God.

Thank you, Most Holy Father, for guiding us on these paths, for enlightening our route with your words, for sustaining us with your prayer and for calling down on us the graces of God through your Apostolic Benediction.

SHARING OF FAITH AS SHARING OF JOY

Speech of the Holy Father to the Plenary Assembly of the Pontifical Council for Dialogue with Non-Believers, 18 March 1991

Your Eminences,
Dear Brother Bishops,
Dear Friends,

1. With joy I receive you this morning and bid you welcome with all my heart. Members and consultors of the Pontifical Council for Dialogue with Non-Believers, you have gathered here in plenary assembly under the presidency of Cardinal Paul Poupard to reflect on a theme that is always timely, with great pastoral significance today: the human longing for happiness as a point of reference for faith. This anthropological approach to faith and, on the other hand, to disbelief, is one of the possible keys for responding better to the dissatisfaction and anguish, the fear and threats which weigh upon people today, and from which they seek to be liberated, in order to open wide to them the door of happiness in the joyous light of the risen Christ, "the one who lives, [the one who] holds the keys of death and the netherworld" (cf. Rv 1:18), the only one who has a definitive answer to people's anguish and despair.
I want to thank you for having proposed the topic of happiness for the reflection of the Church as a meeting place on the path of faith.

2. What is the search for happiness today? What are its characteristics?

From what we can see from the results of the survey published three years ago in your periodical, *Atheism and Faith*, among the traditional peoples of the Third World the desire for happiness is a harmonious insertion in the family and ethnic group and a basic level of material well-being. By contrast happiness is equated with individualism in the affluent societies marked by secularism and religious indifference. Your attention was not only turned to these societies because they have the most non-believers; freedom is often seen in them as a faculty of absolute self-determination exempt from every law. For many people, happiness is no longer connected with the fulfilment of a moral duty, nor with the search for a personal relationship with God. In this sense, we can speak of a split between happiness and morality. Seeking happiness in virtue thus becomes a foreign ideal, and even strange to a number of our contemporaries. They are moved by interest in their body, health, beauty and youth. It is the image of happiness hemmed in by the vicious circle of desire and its satisfaction. It is true that compassion, good will towards others and true generosity, even among those who are distant from the faith, are also characteristic of these societies.

This culture is also described as narcissistic. The myth invented by the ancient Greeks shows how the ancients already were aware of the sterility of a love closed in upon itself. Loving only one's self is self-destruction and death. "Whoever wishes to save his or her life", Jesus says, "will lose it" (Mk 8:35).

Concern for others and forgetting one's self because of that concern for the other person and his or her well-being: are not these the most expressive images of the divine mystery? The living and true God, whom Jesus revealed to us, is not a solitary God. Among the divine Persons everything is made a gift, sharing, communication, in an eternal expression of love. All God's happiness and joy are the happiness and joy of mutual giving. For the human being, made in God's image, there is no true joy except in giving one's self. "Whoever loses his or her life for my sake and that of the Gospel will save it" (Mk 8:35), says Jesus.

3. Another consideration is necessary. Unlike the ancients who had a very poignant understanding of life, of the human being's loneliness in the world, of our inadequacy before the ideals of beauty and goodness, of the fleeting nature of all things, and lastly of the fatality of existence, the production-oriented consumer society refuses to integrate the presence and experience of evil and death into its idea of happiness. It makes of this fact an image of fragile, artificial and, ultimately, false happiness. Every system that does not plumb the depths of this sombre enigma of life has very little to say to people, and sooner or later they will reject it. Recent history is proof of this.

4. The Christian concept of life – and happiness – has its source in Jesus Christ, God made man, in his earthly life in our midst, in his death freely accepted and his victory over death on Easter morning. "The mystery of the human person", the Second Vatican Council affirms, "is truly understood only in the mystery of the incarnate Word" (*Gaudium et spes*, 22). The mystery of human happiness has its key in Jesus Christ, the prototype of all life that is given. Jesus Christ abolishes the tragic antagonism between heaven and earth, the present and future, between God and mankind. This time, filled as it is with the effects of sin and yet already ransomed by Christ, can be lived as a time of happiness in the hope of its ultimate fulfilment. This world, where evil and death still reign, can be loved in joy because the Kingdom of God, which will reach its fulfilment when the Lord comes in glory, is already present on this earth (cf. *Gaudium et spes*, 39.3), thus constituting the first draft, the figure and the prophecy of the new heavens and the new earth. Physical reality can be accepted with the weight of all its misery and suffering; death itself can be accepted without despair because of the promise of the resurrection. Everything is redeemed, even the banality of daily life, even the most painful experience. The sinner is always offered forgiveness. This is the Christian meaning of happiness, the promise of the Beatitudes, whose light we want to let shine "like a lamp shining in a dark place until the day begins to dawn and the morning star rises in our hearts" (2 P 1:19).

5. This year the bicentenary of Mozart's death calls our attention to the message of joy found in his work; in it there is a feeling of happiness as a simultaneous experience of death and resurrection. Many people find in it, especially in his religious compositions, a veritable song of joy of the creation which has been redeemed and reconciled with God, an echo of grace, an inexhaustible spring. Sharing the faith must also become a sharing of joy. Dialogue, which all too often becomes an arid exchange of ideas, can find a privileged inspiration in wonder in the presence of artistic beauty, a reflection of God's eternal, indescribable beauty.

6. Dear friends, this plenary assembly on the desire for happiness marks a threshold crossed in your brief but very significant history; it is proper for you to give an anthropological orientation to your reflection. Three years ago you affirmed that the atheistic ideologies and views of the world constructed in the nineteenth century now have only a very limited influence, and the classics of atheism are no longer at centre stage. Militant atheism, because of its ravages, seems to have engendered a new pagan philosophy, that is, the temptation to self-divinisation, as old as Genesis itself, the arbitrary rejection of the moral law, and finally the tragic experience of evil. The industrialised societies with their advanced technology and mentalities conditioned by the media are prey to the depreciation of values and the loss of a moral sense. This is the new terrain for dialogue with non-believers, a task that is more necessary than ever.

7. An era of dialogue freed from the weight of ideologies is opening up the dawn of a new millennium. I am grateful that, through the meetings you have with your collaborators in the different parts of the world, you make the Church aware of this aspect of her mission. Continue this work with patience and discerment, invoking the assistance of the Holy Spirit and the protection of the Virgin Mary, "cause of our joy".
My blessing and prayer are with you in this difficult but necessary task.

WORKS OF CARDINAL POUPARD IN ENGLISH:

What Catholics believe today: an inspired summary of Catholic Doctrine and life today, Dimension Books, Denville, 1970

Galileo Galilei, Toward a Resolution of 350 years of Debate 1633-1983, Duquesne University Press, Pittsburgh, 1987

Translations in the Press:

The Church before the Challenge of Culture, Catholic Central Union of America, St Louis

Christianity and Culture in Europe, Franciscan University Press, Steubenville

God and Freedom, Paulist Press, New York

Most recent publications:

In Italian: *Guida a Roma*, Piemme, 1991

In French: *Dieu et la liberté,* Mame, 1992